Empath

A Practical Healing Guide for Empaths and Highly Sensitive People: Learn How to Stop Absorbing Negative Energies, Regain Your Clarity and Break Free from Narcissistic Entanglements!

Table of Content

The Answers are Coming!

Dear Empath, I'm so happy to be gifting you this book! I hope it will answer some of your questions and bring you comfort, reassurance and practical tools for maintaining greater levels of emotional balance and mental clarity. As an empath, you might sometimes feel as if you're not living life to the fullest, because a great deal of your time is spent *managing* life rather than simply enjoying it!

Dealing with the gut-wrenching thud of self-centred people and their intentions, agendas and manipulations, the nauseating taste of social injustices and the pain they cause in society, the sweat-inducing jangle of financial pressures, in a world that sometimes makes it unbearable to open your eyes in the morning, let alone go out and face the madness of a rush-hour commute and several days , weeks, months, even years of toxic, vampiric office politics, and other people's anger, frustration and disappointment.

Oppressive corporate power-plays, the global climate of fear, the threat of seemingly endless terrors and a plethora of vulnerabilities that other people seem to be able to cope with effortlessly. Except, as an empath, you know this isn't true. You know in your heart that they're not coping at all. They're simply stuffing down their vulnerabilities with alcohol, TV, fine dining, chain-smoking and holidays, but under your intrepid and reluctantly psychic microscope, these vulnerabilities and anxieties are literally oozing out of them, from every quantum pore. And every single one of them, sensing your lightness, is endlessly reaching out to you with decomposing zombie-flesh hands, begging you to clean them up, calm them down, turn them around, fix them up, listen, comfort and cajole or just scoop them up into your arms and give them a whole new life, while your own life is barely held together by threads.

But you love, and you love, and you love, and your heart literally aches, from too many news reports showing starvation, stabbings, sterility and all the other cruelties that human beings inflict upon each other. Alcoholics and homeless people, horror scenes that suddenly appear in PG rated movies, dark energetic oppression from political agendas, panic attacks at the London Dungeon, climbing suicide rates, parental pressures, people with severe illnesses, all tugging, and tugging and tugging at your heart strings. Palpitations and digestive remonstrations, is it you, is it them? Whose feelings are you feeling? Why the sudden headache? Attempting to resolve it all, trying to take away the woes of the world and feeling absolutely irritated when people ask: *why you don't just stop doing it then*!!

And there you are, dear empath, trying to manage it all, without the vocabulary, the support, or the energy to keep explaining to bewildered friends and family, why you *have* to sit in the back row at the cinema and why you *can't* just randomly flat-share with random people or do a random, regular job. Even a grocery shopping trip needs careful planning. Then you start to worry about how much they're all worrying about you, to the point where there's no energy left to even feel annoyed with them for just, so completely failing to understand you, because now you can *feel* them worrying about you.. and that's somehow even more annoying...and draining!

And then, here come people like me, typing away in our cosy little futons, telling you how much the world needs you now, and what a great gift your empathy is. Ah yes, you think to yourself, as you stuff down another bar of chocolate: empathy, the gift that keeps on taking. *But*, beautiful empath, that's all about to change. *Yes*, the world needs your love, and your compassion, and all the wonderful gifts you bring, but you also need a break. You need to know that you're not crazy – the 3d *world* is crazy. You need to know that you can and will have a life you can love, and you need to make sense of all this clawing, gnawing, suffocating, debilitating, life-wrecking, heart-stopping, cock–blocking empathy that stops you having any semblance of a normal life. You need to get out more, savour life again, and have the occasional energy holiday or psychic day off. You need tips, tricks, and maybe even a few downright unorthodox secrets for keeping your precious energy-field toxin and agenda-free, long enough to figure out who you are, what you want and why it really *is* pretty cool being you after all!

Empathy is the future. I believe the new Earth will be filled with empaths and that present-day empaths are simply the ones who decided to go ahead early in order to usher in the new consciousness and pick up some essential multidimensional skills along the way, so that we could become the great teachers and healers we're destined to be.

So, once again, thank you for reading this book and thank you for being here. You are exactly what the world needs at this incredible time and your journey to self-mastery continues here. As you read through this book, I hope you will gradually become aware of the great gift you have been given and the great gift that you are to the world. When you begin to use your gifts more consciously, you will realise that what you have at your fingertips is the ability to manifest heaven on Earth and to see, sense and feel it taking shape before your very eyes.

I hope that as you read on, you will begin to see your deep compassion and empathy for the great blessings they are, and that the tools in this book will help you to awaken fully, and step out into the world once again, with a smile on your face and a new spring in your step. There's nothing wrong with you, and one day you may finally come to see that you were all right, all along.

What is an Empath?

So, what is an empath and why are there suddenly so many of them? Well, before I go into that, let me just stress that a great deal of what follows is only my opinion, based on what I have experienced myself as an empath, a spiritual guide and teacher and someone who has studied for decades, the many worlds and dimensions in which we operate mentally, emotionally, vibrationally and physically.

If I answer the second question first, (why are there suddenly so many of them?) it will help us to place the first question (what is an empath?) into a wider context and to see it from a greater perspective. I believe there are many more empaths on Earth now for many reasons, but the main and perhaps the most important reason is the ascension process we are currently experiencing here on planet Earth. The shift we are currently experiencing was predicted by many ancient cultures and civilisations, who recorded, spoke of and even painted pictures to share news of, a time when the Earth would rise in vibrational frequency and return to an earlier state of higher resonance, peace, love and harmony.

There are many peculiar and noteworthy phenomena which accompany this time and herald our passing from one age into another: a rise in global, political unrest; an increase in inspiring collective movements, spiritual groups and communities; news of polar shifts and spiritual awakenings, and several scientific discoveries which border on the metaphysical and ultimately point our way back to a far more divine and mystical focus for our future belief systems.

The Divine plan for this new age has been many aeons in the making, and over the last few decades, there has been a noticeable shift in consciousness on earth. All around us we see change - change in political structures, attitudes, spirituality, major institutions, our approach towards the environment and this precious land upon which we live. Even within ourselves, many of us are now experiencing change at a rapid pace, and to hear people speaking openly about 'vibes' or openly discussing their vision boards we no longer have to be attending one of our beloved spiritual workshops. The language has penetrated the populous, energy-clearing is being touted in high profile fashion magazines as the latest beauty treatment, everyone seems to be talking about karma, and there are lightworkers everywhere! In fact, it's probably only a matter of time before we see one in government, despite all current appearances.

So, what has triggered all this change and where do empaths fit into it? Well, as most people reading this book will already know, the change has been triggered simply by the Divine Plan for the Earth to ascend at this time, and has been assisted and accelerated by the millions of lightworkers who have been visiting this planet for centuries, in order to assist in the evolution of human consciousness in preparation for this event.

In fact, there are many lightworkers here on the planet right now. You may already know this and absolutely know that you, yourself, are a lightworker as well as an empath. Lightworkers come in all shapes, sizes, colours, races, creeds, job descriptions and vibrational frequencies, and each one of us has our own divinely ordained role to play in this current evolution. Each one of us provides this great shift with a useful function or a helpful vibration, in order to quicken and support the enormous change taking place. In this sense, empaths belong more to the future world than the current one. Their sensitivity is of a fifth dimensional, crystalline nature. In other words, they feel, absorb, respond to and transmute frequency far more than they respond to physical matter, presented facts or speech.

Most empaths experience frequency much more than sensory input, and this is where it gets tricky. While the Earth is still in this strange transitional stage, bouncing around between the 3rd, 4th and 5th dimensions, empaths, who carry the sensitivity of the fifth dimension, can struggle to thrive amid the chaos, simply because they are so sensitive to the lower frequencies of all the chaos, which exists in the 3rd and lower 4th dimensions.

This brings me to the second question, what is an empath? An empath is someone who has the ability to feel the motivations, emotions, and even the thoughts of others. When they look at a person, place or thing, they see beyond its presenting reality. When they listen, they don't simply hear the words that are spoken, they feel every nuance of meaning, vibration and feeling behind them. Some see it as a gift, others - a curse.

Whichever way we choose to view our empathic gifts, we empaths are here in droves, to seed the earth with this new, loving, light frequency and to support others who will one day inevitably ascend into the same level of sensitivity. You may have heard the expression: *show me your friends and I'll tell you who you are.* Well, this simple maxim is hinting at a far greater truth than simple judgement by association. One that stretches far beyond any observations we might make about our tendency to like people who are similar to ourselves. It also speaks of a deeper, metaphysical truth, which states that all beings and all things are constantly seeking to come into vibrational resonance with each other. There is not one thing in the universe that exists in isolation. This is one of the reasons people love spending time with empaths. Empaths are like little packages of love. Little, loving, non-judgemental, rays of light, breaths of fresh air, light seeds, sent here by divine appointment, in order to be cleaners of the old frequency and place holders for the new Earth vibration.

People who spend a lot of time in the company of an empath will ultimately experience a rise in frequency, as a result of proximity. Over time, they will be forced to elevate their frequency into the love vibration, which is the natural set point for the empath. Unfortunately for the empath, this process doesn't always feel so great and certainly doesn't always happen within a reasonable time period, nevertheless, the seed is often sown within the consciousness of those who are in regular contact with an empath, and may even sprout and take root at a much later time, long after the empath has ceased to be in contact with the person or people in question. Nevertheless, they have been impregnated, and their inevitable rebirth is only a matter of time.

The friends, partners, and even the families of empaths may not understand them, and this can compound their feelings of confusion and isolation. Sometimes it may seem as if *you* are the only one who understands you, and this is why it's important to seek out others who are the same as you. This will make it easier for you to have your feelings validated and to be less overwhelmed by those feelings of isolation and deep inner loneliness that many empaths feel on some level. The only problem is that so many empaths are too busy giving their precious time and energy away to unhealed or unpleasant people, to ever manage to find each other.

Empaths need to make a concerted effort to find each other in the kinds of places where empaths enjoy spending time. You won't find many empaths hanging out in nightclubs or at parties. Parties are no fun for empaths – too many people to clean, all in one room! The last party I attended wasn't even a party, it was a theatre show in a school. It was a fun show, and everyone seemed to be enjoying themselves, but I was surrounded by overworked and unhappy teachers who couldn't wait to rip into the rare boxes of end of term wine. After sitting in their company for a few hours, absorbing the repressed rage and desperation which was deftly hidden beneath the light-hearted teacher banter about the stresses of the job, I wanted to go to the bathroom and dry heave for hours and then sleep for a week. However, neither of these things would have been polite or practical at the time, so I excused myself as early as possible and combined energy-clearing and moderate sleep with a bit of a demoralised go-slow at work for the next couple of days, and vowed never to be talked into any more socialising! That was a long time ago, however, and the tools and techniques I'll share with you later in this book have been truly life-changing in allowing me to feel more comfortable in some social situations. As a general rule, though, for empaths, what looks to everyone else like a pleasant evening of socialising can easily turn into an entire week of lost focus, a headache, a stomach-ache or any number of other physical, mental or emotional upsets.

Empaths Never Stop Working. We *are* the job!

Whether they know it or not, empaths are the workaholics of the lightworker tribe, because they literally never stop working. Almost everyone and everything can represent a new energy-clearing opportunity or project, and there are only so many hours in the day. Let me just add here, that the work doesn't necessarily even stop during the day, and I'm sure I'm not the only empath who has to be careful where I sleep, and who remains aware of every breath and every twist and turn of everyone in the house. I know when people have woken up, not only because I hear them, but because I feel them... sometimes I feel them plugging into my energy for the day ahead, or, depending who they are, sometimes I might also get a nice surprise in discovering that they're feeling happy about the day ahead, and are even thinking pleasant thoughts about our time together. Good times!

Because the empath is always unconsciously trying to bring balance and resonance between ourselves and others, if there is an illness, an unhealthy consciousness, a lower energy vibration, a deep density, a depression or even a bottomless soul sickness, the empath will naturally, automatically (whether consciously or unconsciously) 'go there' energetically, in a desperate attempt to fix it, heal it, cleanse it, clear it or otherwise engage with it, and order restore it to its highest vibrational potential. And sometimes, that whole process just isn't very much fun for the empath! In fact, sometimes it's utterly debilitating! But such is the job of the empath, and this job needs to be managed, structured and organised, so that we can become the empowered and effective healers we came here to be, whilst also maintaining some sanity and stability in our own lives.

So, I've said it before, but I think it's worth repeating: if you are an empath, you are not wrong, or weird, or broken. You are everything that's right in the world and here's where you get to figure out why, and how you can make it all work for you!

Are Empaths Born or Created?

If you are an empath who has struggled a great deal to understand your gift, your temperament and your funny little quirks and needs, you might have asked yourself the question, why am I like this!!!? Members of your family might have asked you similar questions, making you feel even more anxious, misunderstood, broken and, ultimately, somehow wrong for being the way you are. In a sense, even the question about whether empaths are born or created implies that there's something wrong with empaths and that everyone else is normal.

So, here's my question to you: apart from the horrible pain that can sometimes be caused by your incredible sensitivity, which do you think the world currently needs most: more incredibly insensitive people or more sensitive, compassionate and nurturing people? Can you honestly say that in an insanely insensitive world, continuing to be insensitive is the best way for humanity to progress? Surely, we've been doing that for long enough now! It's time for something else, something new. So, personally, my current feeling is that however many times I may be told I'm too sensitive, too kind, too soft, too caring, I refuse to accept that all these fine and beautiful qualities are a mistake!

This is what I want for you too, dear empath. By the time we get to the end of this book, I want you to feel ready to march out into the world like the strong, proud, light-bearer you are, and to enjoy every minute of the ascending Earth light-show, of which you are an essential and integral part. No more sitting on the side-lines with popcorn, wishing everyone would just leave you alone. It's time to integrate your 5th dimensional magic with your human heart, mind, body and soul and become the powerful light seed you know you were always destined to be.

When we come into the world, I believe we enter with many soul contracts and agreements, designed with a great many potential learning opportunities in mind. Some of us are simply born extremely sensitive, depending on our soul's development or the dimensions in which we have accrued most of our soul's development. There are many souls on Earth who have spent most of their incarnations in places where the energies and polarities are far less harsh than here on Earth. Earth is a tough assignment. Therefore, when sensitive souls from other dimensions incarnate here in service to the earth, it is a true labour of love. You might call these beings Earth angels, starseeds, indigos, crystal children, avatars or any number of other names given to lightworkers, and I believe that many early empaths fall into one or more of these categories.

Many of these lightworker empaths are born into families where the genetic history contains certain character and personality sensitivities and fragilities, conscious or unconscious, with a view to making these things conscious and flooding them with healing light, for the highest good of all. This can be seen in the case of empaths who are born to narcissistic parents.

Other empaths are created, for example, many empaths were neglected or abused as children and, as a result, they may have become hyper vigilant about their own safety and security or the moods, feelings, ups and downs and emotional needs of others. Some empaths, for example those who grew up in violent households, may have found themselves growing up in situations where they would literally have to make sure everyone else was feeling okay before they would be able to relax. If an unpredictably violent parent was known for lashing out when they were unhappy, a nervous child might develop empathic or even psychic skills, as a means of self-preservation – in other words, developing skills that would allow them to see trouble coming. For this reason, many empaths who were abused or neglected as children will become overly concerned with the welfare of everyone else, still unable to feel good until everyone else is feeling good.

Other empaths might develop their sensitivities in a loving and supportive home, in which they are allowed to simply be themselves, even if this means being introverted, shy and quiet, and perhaps developing unusual artistic talents. So, there is no simple answer to the question of whether empaths are born or made. However, one thing all empaths seem to have in common is that they feel things very deeply and need plenty of time alone to rest and recharge. Because they are so vulnerable to shifts and changes in emotional, mental and energetic temperature, empaths must absolutely develop a strong, self-loving inner culture of self-belief, and a routine attitude of deep self-care and unshakeable self-respect.

Whether you feel you were born an empath or have become one as a result of a spiritual awakening, a childhood trauma or a desire to be of service to the world, we are all here to perform the same function, and that is what matters most.

The Difference between a Sensitive Person and an Empath

A highly sensitive person is very similar to an empath. They may also feel desperately uncomfortable in crowded places and over-stimulated by events happening in the world. They may feel lonely and misunderstood for much of the time and may often see their sensitivity as a curse. The main difference between empaths and sensitive people is that empaths can sense, feel and experience the feelings, emotions and motivations of others, whereas sensitive people don't necessarily possess this added element of a psychic and extra sensory nature.

If you're extremely sensitive, it might be difficult to know whether you are also an empath. Sometimes it's much easier to know that you're sensitive than it is to know precisely *how* you're sensitive.

Similar to an empath, a sensitive person might also avoid spending too much time with too many people, because along with people comes a great deal of information and stimuli, which they'll need to process later, however, they might not be actually experiencing the emotions of those people.

If you are an empath, you might also be empathic with more than just people. You might feel the pain of animals, the thoughts of plants, the emanations that come from violent, creepy or frightening paintings. You might be deeply hurt by some of the energies you feel coming from someone who claims to love you. You might experience a punching feeling in the stomach when someone close to you has an envious thought about you while smiling at you magnanimously.

When someone else is ill, depressed or suffering, a sensitive person might be able to comfort them by knowing exactly what to say to make them feel better, by giving them a warm, loving hug, or demonstrating understanding of what they must be going through. But an empath will feel ill on their behalf or become completely debilitated by unconsciously attempting to balance their energy for them. A sensitive person needs to avoid over-stimulating situations, people and places in order to feel whole, whereas an empath needs to fix and heal everything and everyone around them before they can feel better.

For a long time, I thought I was just very sensitive, or even "too sensitive." I hadn't heard of empaths. I didn't know why my stomach was always tied up in knots when I was close to certain people – most people! I had no idea why I needed to spend so much time alone. It was crazy how little I went out. For a very long time this absurd sensitivity felt like a huge burden. In fact, I didn't even know what 'it' was. I knew I felt different, behaved weirdly and probably wasn't 'normal'. I knew people probably thought I was weird. I knew the world was sometimes excruciatingly painful for me in a way that it didn't seem to be for everyone else. I often had unexplained stomach pains, needed to be alone, worried excessively and felt anxious for no particular reason. I just knew on some level that I had to make sure everyone else was happy before I could be happy, and I knew I would have to keep stepping aside compliantly, allowing everyone else to take the promotions, gifts, opportunities and good times, not because I was a doormat, but because I could feel the people standing on the other side of those lovely things pulling and tugging at me, psychically attacking or energetically manipulating me, and at some point I usually decided that it just wasn't worth arguing if they wanted those things so badly. I just energetically didn't have the stomach for a fight. If other people felt bad, I felt bad, so I certainly wasn't about to set up a conflict situation... As long as they were okay and had what they wanted, they would leave me alone in peace, and everyone would get what they wanted, well, almost!

Empaths often get drawn into long conversations with energy vampires who will target and corner them, often attempting to keep them in close proximity, as a source of energy supply. In most cases, the empath will feel compelled to stay in position, sensing the energy vampire's deep need, and feeling obliged to stand there listening, and listening ....and listening.... A sensitive person won't necessarily feel all these nuances of psychic interaction, and they might find it easier to leave the scene more quickly than an empath would. Highly sensitive people don't necessarily feel the same sense of obligation or the desperate need to heal everything and everyone, however, they can also become just as drained and exhausted by toxic and negative interactions.

Are You an Empath?

By now, you'll have a reasonable idea of what an empath is and how they might experience life. You might have come to this book knowing that you're an empath but looking for confirmation, and for reassurance that you're not going crazy. Knowing whether you're an empath can be the first step towards healing, because in recognising yourself, you can move towards greater levels of self-acceptance, rather than fighting within yourself and feeling confused and embarrassed about who you are.

When we truly accept ourselves, along with all our quirks, preferences and unique personal needs, we can not only find greater peace within ourselves, but we can also finally begin to release trying to get others to understand, sympathise or appreciate our gifts. Empowered with a new understanding about ourselves, we can begin to connect with others who are the same and seek out the tools and techniques we need to keep ourselves energetically clear, vibrant, balanced and happy.

If you are an unconscious empath, you might have spent your entire life feeling confused, strange, misunderstood and being thrown off balance by the tiniest of insults and the seemingly most meaningless incidents. You might have spent days, weeks, months or even years recovering from careless comments and put downs that others might have brushed aside in an instant. You might have felt vulnerable, weak and, at times, even emotionally disabled in the world, and there may have even been times when you have questioned your own sanity. You might have attracted many unscrupulous people who preyed upon your vulnerabilities or who, for their own reasons, somehow managed to convince you that you are unstable, unwise or unrealistic. But here is where all that stops! It's time for you to take ownership of your gift, along with its many idiosyncrasies, and to fully appreciate the wonderful creative, spiritual and life-affirming benefits that your precious vulnerabilities bring. And the first step in healing any wounded thoughts you may currently be holding about yourself, is to recognise who and what you are.

Read the statements below and see how many of them resonate with you and your own experiences of sensitivity. Make a note of how many times you answer yes. If you answer yes to more than fifteen statements, it's more than likely that you are an empath.

1. Do you often feel confused about who you are and what you want, when you find yourself in the company of certain people?

2. Do you change your mind frequently – maybe several times a day - about major decisions, depending on the opinions of others and what you sense they might want for you?

3. Do you feel the pain of others – either emotional, physical or in the form of mental anxiety and confusion?

4. Do you put others first, allowing them to have the best lives, get the best promotions, steal opportunities from under your nose and even leave you broke?

5. Do you over-give just to keep everyone else happy?

6. Do you often accept less than you deserve because it means staying safe energetically?

7. Have your finances suffered in an y way because you fear being overwhelmed by the energies of other people?

8. Do you often enter intimate relationships with broken people, and feel it's your job to fix them?

9.   Have you ever been involved in a toxic relationship with a narcissist or any other kind of abusive partner?

10. Do you tend to overstay in relationships that hurt you because you don't want to hurt someone else's feelings, or because you believe you can change them for the better?

11. Do you find it hard to say no?

12. Are you a great listener who always knows what to say to make people feel better?

13. Do you often feel overwhelmed, emotionally or mentally?

14. Do you often experience physical symptoms such as headaches and stomach aches after spending time with negative people?

15. Do you feel the true feelings, thoughts and motivations of others, even when they try to disguise them with smiles, wiles or cleverness?

16. Do you avoid listening to the news and watching creepy films because you feel their impact physically?

17. Are you generally very intuitive and able to sense energies?

18. Do you find it easy to sense the energies in a room?

19. Do you prefer spending time alone to being with people?

20. Do you often feel drained and tired without knowing why?

21. Do you avoid crowded events, gatherings and places at all costs?

22. Do you absorb the feelings of others, for example becoming depressed after spending time with depressed people?

23. Do you sometimes continue to spend time with people even though you sense they may be deceiving you?

24. Do you have strong gut feelings or unpleasant physical and energetic symptoms, when in the presence of someone envies you or who doesn't have your best interests at heart?

25. Do you sometimes experience the physical symptoms of sick people when you spend time with them?

26. Are you often told you're too sensitive?

27. Are you sometimes accused of being reclusive or told you need to get out more?

The Many Gifts of Empathy

If you've read this far, I think we can assume you're an empath, so let's take a deep breath and take a moment to celebrate you!! Yes, that's right, I did say celebrate!

So far in this book we've explored a lot of the not-so-great things about what it can mean to be an empath. The sticky, icky things, the *oh my God, why can't I just be normal* things. It's pretty heavy stuff, right? So, before we continue to explore these things in greater depth, I thought it would be nice to look at some of the amazing benefits gifted to us as empaths, as well as the things that make us such an incredible gift to the world.

As an empath, you might have noticed that you are a creature who feels a great number of things in a great deal of depth, in glorious technicolour, breathtaking cinemascope and stereophonic sound. You're able to experience the world in such depth it sometimes defies reason. When you breathe deeply while standing high on a hill, you taste the sweet and rarefied air, when you listen to beautiful music, you experience it as it was written, feeling all the composer's emotion and intention. When you love, you love completely, truly madly, deeply, usually enough for both people. Okay, that one isn't so great because it often means you find it almost impossible to notice when you're not also *receiving* love in return. You are such a complete, all-in, all-inclusive bubble of love that what you often mistake for a loving relationship is sometimes simply your own abundant, self-generated love, flowing, growing and glowing all around you. Nevertheless, that love is yet another of your many gifts. Not everyone feels love this deeply or to such a great extent. In fact, so many of the things we as empaths take for granted are not necessarily experienced by others. This doesn't make us any better than they are, just different.

Here are some of the wonderful gifts that often come as a direct result, or a pleasant side-benefit, of your natural empathy.

Creativity!

Because of their ability to feel so deeply and to express such depth of feeling, many empaths are also very gifted artists and creatives.

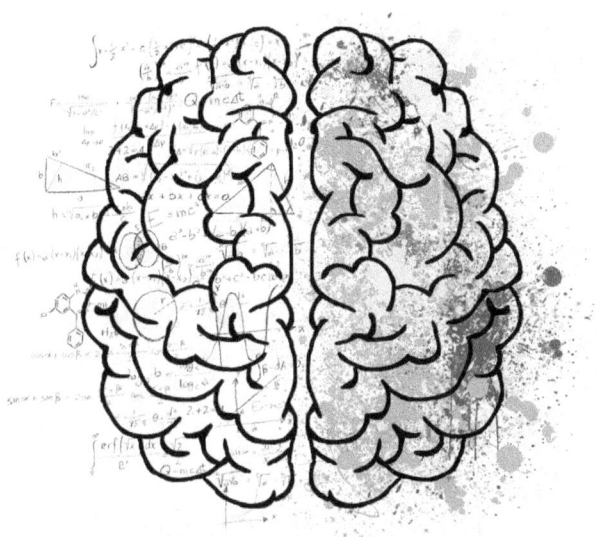

If you're one of those people, please don't ever belittle your creative gifts or take them for granted again. Be grateful for the painful empathy that makes you such a powerfully inspired artist. Your creativity is like a portal into a beautiful new world. Your music/paintings/cake decorating/cookery and baking/fashion-sense/fashion-design/knitting/sewing skills/chocheting/dancing/acting/writing/musicianship/song-writing/poetry or other form of creative self-expression is a portal into the 5th dimension and a vehicle through which the most indescribably beautiful stream of Divine love travels and is seeded into the world. Treasure your creativity and value it, along with all the sensitivity that allows you access to it. Treasure these things with all your empathic, loving heart! You are here to make miracles of love!

Healing

Because of their incredible ability to feel and discern the feelings, thoughts and even the physical symptoms of others, empaths make wonderful healers of all kinds. Learning to be a healer will take a great deal of discipline for empaths, as it will be absolutely necessary for them to learn how to separate themselves from the people they serve and treat, in order to maintain healthy levels of vitality and balance within themselves. These gifts of energy management will be essential as we continue to ascend, and increased sensitivity and spiritual awakenings become more commonplace.

Most empaths who become healers will be adept at working with energy and do extremely well when working with complementary therapies which are based on vibrational principles, such as Reiki, Cosmo-energetics, Theta-healing, and a vast array of other quantum techniques for transformation. As the planetary shift gathers momentum, empaths who are also healers will become increasingly valued, and even though you may not yet be able to see or fully understand this, there will come a time when your skills are called upon frequently. When this time arrives, make sure you are fully prepared and ready and able to carry out the job you came here to do, in service to humanity. Learning how to clear and protect your energy will not only enable you to live a happier and more fulfilled life, it will also prepare you for this role of planetary service.

Because of their incredible listening skills and their sixth sensory ability to see below the surface of what's being verbalised, empaths also make incredible psychotherapists or mind-based practitioners of all kinds. In fact, anyone who is seeking to understand themselves better, heal childhood wounds or discover what prevents them from becoming happy, can rely on an empath to get them there faster. And, as long as they are willing to give back to themselves and take the time to meditate on these things, empaths can also use these gifts to discern what's stopping or blocking them from moving ahead in life and achieving happiness.

Psychic Ability and Intuition

Because most empaths are psychic, they can be extremely insightful in helping others to understand their life-path and make wiser decisions based on the vibrational information or Divine inspiration that empaths will be able to feel or discern on their behalf. Although many empaths have a habit of not using this gift for their own benefit in guiding their own lives – usually because they're too busy worrying about what others might want for them – when it comes to guiding and assisting others, they can be alarmingly incisive and will identify the source of problems or blockages with laser-like precision.

As an empath, you are also gifted with an acute sense of responsibly and ethics. For you, doing the right thing doesn't simply mean following rules and guidelines, it also means being aware of how energy flows and feels and therefore understanding, only too well, the karmic ramifications of incorrect thoughts, careless words or faulty information and guidance. These things will trouble an empathy deeply, because we don't just *believe* that every action creates an effect, we also feel these effects long before they are created into physical form. If you go to an empath for an intuitive reading, they will always guide you back to your own wisdom. They will never tell you bad things are going to happen, because they honour and recognise your authority as the creator of your own experience. You will never have one of those creepy, debilitating or worrying readings from an empath, because they will always be feeling what you're feeling, and wanting to make sure you leave feeling better than you did before you came to see them.

Empaths who work as psychics and intuitives should also try to extend the same kindness towards ourselves, always endeavouring to remain within the vibrational current where *all is well*. As an empath, you will immediately know if something is 'off' about a person, their energy, or the way you feel after spending time with them, and we need to make a frequent practice of checking in with ourselves to see what has pulled us out of the vibrant stream of well-being and positive expectation. This is a great gift! There are many people wondering through the world, carrying its weight on their shoulders, unaware of the incremental acquisition of these woes. As an emapth, you can feel these cares piling on, minute, to minute and banish them before they can have an impact on your general health, well-being, attitude and mental clarity.

The Feel-Good Factor

Just as easily as empaths are able to pick up on and feel toxic and undesirable vibrations, they are also able to experience the good ones! Observe a fellow empath enjoying a sunset, an ice-cream, a Jacuzzi, a massage, a walk in the sunshine or the rain, a warm hug, a cuddle in front of a good movie, essential oils or good food, and you'll see someone who knows how to really enjoy life! Remember, lovely empath, just as intensely as you feel the bad stuff, you can also fully embrace, indulge in, and relish the good stuff like no one else can! And it's important to surround yourself with good people, good experiences, quality time all to yourself and extreme self-care.

Because empaths are able to feel so good, they can also pass on these good feelings to others. They make great chefs because they can often taste their ideas and creations before they put them into their mouths. And because they've spent so much time studying ways to have the safest and most energetically comfortable social outings, they'll also take you for the best night out ever! An empath will have spent a lot of time researching ways to feel good or feel better. They'll know that your crème caramel will taste better just slightly warm, and home-cooked, they'll lead you to the best little cosy independent cinemas and the nicest places to stroll along the riverbank, the best parks and the most cultural, quiet and unhurried spots in the city – if they still dare to live there! If you're ever lucky enough to be a guest in their home, their dining table will display the most fragrant flowers, the most pristine white candles, and they'll share with you the best way to warm your bathrobe before even stepping into the shower, where you'll find the most scrumptious of naturally scented soaps, the coolest new age music or the best jazz – the kind that doesn't jangle your nerves. And when you step into their home you'll feel as if you've stepped into the best little bohemian chill-out lounge ever.

Dear empath, please remember that all these beautiful gifts of discernment, style, kindness and care must be regularly enjoyed by yourself, and that you'll become even better at your main gifts when you take time to fully recharge and indulge yourself. Try to resist the temptation to only ever focus on recovering from energy-abuse and take time to also rise above the level of mere survival, into the heady heights of feel-good. Remember, the better you feel, the more radiant you'll become and the more wonderful things you'll be able to create, and that includes creating and manifesting a life that feels good to *you* as well as for everyone else.

Sensing Danger

When it comes to new people, new experiences, and the huge variety of possibilities and choices we might come across in life, most empaths are blessed with the ability to see into the heart of things with speed and precision. They have an uncanny knack for seeing through lies and deceit. Where they sometimes go wrong, however, is by also being very suggestible at times. In fact, I've heard many stories of empaths who have fallen for the latest online scam, while knowing all the time that they were being duped, simply because the person selling the scam was so powerfully persuasive and their emanations were so strong, and when it comes down to it, most empaths always want to believe the best about everyone. So, somewhere deep inside, they are secretly hoping their intuitions and insights are wrong. After all, how is it *possible* for anyone to be so mean, deceitful and unjust?!

One of the biggest problems empaths face is their inability to believe that some people are simply cruel. Because empaths are beautiful, pure 5th dimensional souls who are hard-wired to believe that anything can be fixed and anyone can be healed with enough time, love and patience, they are never quite willing to believe they are being deceived, even when these deceptions are staring them in the face. This is another reason empaths are so vulnerable to bullies and narcissists – they always believe these people are just on the brink of a powerful, life-changing transformation.

Empaths who learn to sit with themselves quietly and contemplate what's being offered rather than allowing themselves to be rushed into premature decision-making will be better able to protect themselves from the scams and unscrupulous requests of others. If they take time to listen to what their intuition is screaming at them, they will improve the quality of all their interactions, friendships, intimate relationships, business dealings and career or life decisions.

Another problem sometimes faced by empaths is the fact that they have been told by so many people that their judgement is flawed, that their thinking is incorrect or that their intuitive feelings and impulses are *just their imagination*. And for many empaths, a period of retraining and rebuilding their self-trust may be necessary before they can begin to believe that those little nudges and uneasy feelings are not simply nausea or paranoia, and that they are, in fact, all the reasons we need to step back and reflect on what is happening.

Never, ever allow yourself to be rushed into a decision of any kind, especially when you can sense what's going on under the surface. You are absolutely entitled to say you need more time to think about an offer, and anyone pushing you into making a decision very quickly is a definite red flag! Stop, look, listen, think and take time to re-connect with your deepest truth and your inner knowing about what's really happening. If you feel yourself being drawn into someone else's forceful reality, this is not a decision-making issue, it's an energy-clearing issue. Your decision was already made within the first five seconds of meeting the deceptive person. Stop, wait, listen and clear your energy. Then breathe, relax and completely disregard any thoughts about their disappointment or displeasure. Let it go! You had a lucky escape. You have a supernatural ability to see beyond the veil, use it!

Super-charged Manifestations

Because of their ability to imagine vividly and place themselves in imaginary situations outside of time, space and 3d reality, empaths are naturally gifted at manifestation and the law of attraction. As an empath, you should also find it easy to change your emotional state, because you have spent years, decades and possibly even a lifetime shifting yourself back into a positive vibration after encountering yet another blast of negative energy from the external world. For you, shifting, clearing and raising your frequency comes as naturally as breathing. This doesn't necessarily mean you always find it easy, but you are certainly adept enough at it to have developed the energy mastery required for creating more desirable circumstances in life.

Unfortunately, in order to galvanise the full potential of these gifts, you will have to work hard on removing the negative attachments, traps and influences that usually plague you as an empath, and this may prove to be challenging. However, your gift of psychic insight will help you to recognise what prevents you from achieving your wishes and desires more quickly, therefore allowing you to work on transforming or dissolving these energies. This in another reason why it is essential to avoid input from negative people. Avoid their company as much as possible and seek out positive people who will inspire and encourage you along your path.

Empaths are always on the lookout for people they can fix, so it's quite rare to find an empath who is surrounded by positive, uplifting and inspiring people. This would be a triumph of the healed empath. You will usually see empaths surrounded by vampires, attracting one after another, throughout the course of their lives. In order for empaths to galvanise our potential as energy masters and practitioners of the law of attraction, we must begin to:

- Eliminate negative people from our lives or minimise their influence. In other words, don't ask for their opinion - about anything! Don't share your plans, ideas or insecurities with them and don't spend too much time with them

- Work daily on energy-clearing, to make sure we are beginning our manifesting from a clean slate, free from the sabotaging negative thought forms of envious or disruptive people

- Spend as much time as possible feeling good, doing things we love to do and remaining in a happy and positive state of mind

- Find a circle of positive, happy, focused and motivated people who are also determined to improve their lives

- Learn to receive from life rather than to simply see ourselves as the eternal givers and victims

Once you start implementing those steps and spend time visualising what you want from within this circle of blessings, you'll be amazed at the miracles that will begin to unfold in your life. Then you will see that your life and your abundant gifts truly are a blessing, and you will rise up and see yourself and your life as they truly are!

Why the World Needs Empaths

Empaths are the most wonderfully loving, caring and giving people. They can feel what others are feeling and know exactly what to say or do to make them feel better. As parents, empaths are truly able to sense the needs of their children and to bring them up knowing beyond a shadow of doubt that they are loved beyond measure, even when they misbehave. They, in turn will go on to have healthy relationships in which this circle of love is continued. And this is simply one of the many ways empaths bring more love to the planet.

Everyone whose life is touched by an empath is left somehow better. There is an unconditionally loving quality in the vibration of empaths that feels like a breath of heaven, and because of this, empaths often serve as a much-needed reminder of what it means to be truly human and what it means to be divinely human. When an empath looks into our eyes, holds our hand and or simply listens and deeply understands us, we feel validated and seen. This is something that many hurt or damaged people are lacking in their lives, and because there are now so many empaths on the planet, there are so many more healed hearts than there would have otherwise been.

Because of the empath's high standards of behaviour and ethics, they also serve as a marker, a reminder of more innocent and simple times, when we regarded each other with more kindness and saw these things as important factors of our relating. Empaths are placeholders for old fashioned honesty, kindness and caring.

Empaths are peacemakers. Because most empaths feel conflict and discord in their energy field and find these energies so unbearable to experience, they are always seeking to avoid them by bringing harmony and good feeling between people. Because of their gentle temperament and natural easy-going presence, people generally listen to empaths, and their ability to connect with people from all cultures, belief systems and walks of like without judgement, makes them a valuable peace-keeping element in any work place, family, or situation where there's a potential for discord or strife.

So, if you're in any doubt as to why your presence here on Earth is so essential, you might want to read this chapter and the previous one again. Read them whenever you're in any doubt about the value of your sensitivity and share this book with your friends who are empaths. Hopefully, you will know by now how essential it is that you give yourself the gift of friendship with other empaths! Right?!

Below is a random selection of other beautiful gifts possessed by some empaths. They could be gifts that you, yourself are on the verge of developing. If you have already developed them, you'll find even more to celebrate in the list below.

Many empaths are able to:

- Communicate with animals

- Communicate with plants (and may also have green fingers as a result)

- Sense the energies and consciousness of crystals and essential oils

- See auras

- Extract pain from others without hurting themselves in the process

- Experience telepathy

- Know when loved ones who are several miles away are in need of their help

- Experience altered states of consciousness

- Communicate with angels, fairies, ascended masters and spirit guides

- Sense when the weather is about to change

- Work very powerfully with energy, shaping and changing their reality at will

- Learn new skills extremely quickly by connecting with the spirit of each new gift or program of study

- Access knowledge and information about past lives

- Change the energy frequency of others and bring them into higher vibration

Why Empaths Need Time Alone

If you've spent many years or decades of your life being an empath and being an introvert at the same time, you might not have connected the two things. There are many introverts who are not empaths, so you might have simply believed that your need to spend so much time alone was a symptom of shyness or of generally being a very self-contained person. But, if you're an empath, the truth about your need to be alone maybe more complex than that.

Empaths need time alone to heal from the maelstrom of energies and influences they will encounter in the world on a day-to-day basis. These energies will impact empaths in ways they won't necessarily impact others who are not empaths, sometimes leaving them feeling depleted, overwhelmed, exhausted and misunderstood. In fact, the feeling of being misunderstood can then often cause empaths to feel an even greater sense of loneliness and isolation. However, when left alone to indulge in solo activities they can feel quite contented. This is another factor in the empath's need to be alone. It can be exhausting trying to explain to people the energetic soup we find ourselves swimming in twenty-four seven, and how heavy it can sometimes feel. So rather than repeatedly explaining ourselves and risking disbelief, disrespect and yet again, more misunderstanding, we often find it less toxic and less tiring to simply be alone. In fact, there are times when a blissfully uninterrupted day, spent entirely alone feels like heaven on Earth to an empath.

Many empaths even have trouble sharing a bed at night, as energy never sleeps, and empaths are usually constantly absorbing the energies and emotions of others around them, even when they are 'resting'. As an empath, you may have noticed that you sometimes wake up feeling exhausted after a full night's sleep, or that you open your eyes feeling utterly depressed when you went to sleep feeling perfectly happy! You might find sleepovers difficult, even with intimate partners, and being married or cohabiting on a full-time basis might sometimes feel like a full-time job!

Most of my psychic friends who are fairly empathic tell me they get exhausted and overwhelmed if they see too many clients in a week. They have to open up their energy fields and work with people in a way that can feel very tiring on the energy system. Even though they are channelling Divine energy, the anxiety involved in connecting and interacting so intimately with several different energy fields can be exhausting if they don't take enough rest days and administer quality self-care on their days off. But most empaths don't have days off. For most empaths, there is no opening up and closing down to prepare for a psychic reading; their entire life is one long, ongoing psychic reading. Empaths would benefit greatly from the skills used by professional psychics and intuitives, and I'll share some of these later in the book. I hope they will help you to transform your life in wonderful and unexpected ways.

Empaths need time alone, to not only process the overstimulation that comes from too much contact time, but to relax their energy completely without feeling vulnerable to attack, encroachment or psychic suffocation. It takes time for most people to decompress after stressful situations, but empaths are like psychic sponges who have not only experienced these situations at a mental or emotion level but have also felt and absorbed them and worked hard to process the energy and emotions of everyone involved.

If you frequently experience feelings of emotional or psychic overwhelm, find ways to communicate your needs to those around you. It might be the hardest thing you've ever done, and you might absolutely dread the confusion and ridicule that you imagine will follow, but you might also be pleasantly surprised. People who love us usually want to understand us. They may have been puzzled by our behaviour for years and may struggle to understand why they can never get to spend as much time with us as they'd like to, and why we sometimes behave so strangely when they do!

Opening up to those you love will give them an opportunity to see you as you are and give *you* an opportunity to discover whether those relationships are sustainable in the long-term. Vampiric friends may not respond well to your attempts to put boundaries in place, or to any other attempts to have your needs met. This, in itself, should be useful information for you. Others will simply need time to adjust to what you're saying, if the territory is unfamiliar to them. Until you speak up, there's no way of knowing how your loved ones will respond, but at least you will have begun a journey that allows you to gradually open up to others and stop stuffing your feelings down. In this way, you will allow yourself to receive, and give your loved ones an opportunity to give back to you the thing you treasure and value most – space!

Things That Trigger Empaths into Overwhelm

As we explored earlier, there are many reasons why simply knowing you're an empath can be the first step in your healing journey. However, not all empaths are aware of the various triggers that can cause them to feel overwhelmed and depleted.

We know we don't particularly like being trapped at parties or at noisy gathering. We know that there are days when even the underground can feel toxic. Personally, I always prefer to take a bus when it's an option. There's a weird dark energy in the underground system and, just like me, once down there, the energy doesn't seem to have any means of escape! On the bus, there's fresh air blowing through the windows and things to look at on the streets below, and even though there may be lots of other people around, the passing scenery gives you more interesting things to place your focus on than studiously avoiding eye contact. Even in the cities or large towns there may be the occasional park or tree to connect with telepathically for a quick recalibration. Thank God for the many wonders of nature!

Even in build-up areas, being on a bus can give us a greater sense of space. We can see sights and sounds around us that we wouldn't see on the underground. We can visually engage with a wider field of vision and spread ourselves out a tiny bit more.

So, as the example above demonstrates, sometimes the quirkiest, strangest things can set us off at a moment's notice and avoiding some of the more obvious ones is probably the main reason we manage to remain sane. But just in case you're still questioning yourself and doubting your sanity because of some of the strange choices that come most naturally to you, here are a few of the things I've noticed empaths finding most triggering. I hope that reading the list below will reassure you and encourage you to be kinder to yourself when making decisions about what works or doesn't work for you in the way you live your daily life. I'll also offer some tips that should help you to deal with some of your triggers more successfully.

o **Crowds**

This is possibly the most obvious trigger for most empaths, as it involves coming into contact with the energies of so many different people all in one complicated blast. Most of them will usually be strangers, and therefore carry energies that will be completely unknown to the empath. As empaths, we can be very picky about who we choose to spend time with. We have to be extremely careful not to spend too much time with people who are carrying a huge backlog of unprocessed emotion or whose energy field is full of toxic and draining attachments.

When we enter a crowded room, we're a bit like Forest Gump with his blessed box of chocolates: we truly never know what we're going to get. Even at the most beautiful spiritual events, we can't afford to take anything for granted, and we can almost certainly expect to find a mixed bag of energies just about anywhere!

After being in a crowd of any sort, many empaths will often feel exhausted from managing such a voluminous range of energies in one sitting and will sometimes need to take a salt bath, conduct energy-clearing exercises and get to bed early.

- ○ **Enclosed Spaces**

Enclosed spaces can be a huge trigger for empaths, even when they only contain a handful of people. There are times when even one unhealed person can become a problem for an emotional empath and being trapped in a lift or a car with an energy-vampire for example can feel like sheer torture. When faced with these possibilities, many empaths will opt for the stairs or public transport, knowing only too well the feelings of exhaustion and disappointment that will be waiting for them on the top floor or at the end of the cab ride.

Not all empaths are triggered by confined spaces, however, and the empaths who do have reservations about them are more concerned about the people they will be sharing these confined spaces with, rather than the spaces themselves, and, once again, the feeling of having no escape from a mixed bag of energies. So, this trigger shouldn't be confused with claustrophobia. Any empath who happily takes the lift to the fourteenth floor every day for several years, only to one day become trapped inside it with the office vampire, will be quick to point out the difference.

Emotional Suffocation and Possessiveness

Most empaths struggle in romantic relationships, even those with the most kind and considerate of partners. Whether they know it or not, many people who are attracted to empaths are drawn to their sweet, unconditionally loving, non-judgemental nature. They like being close to them. It feels good. Empaths are natural nurturers and often channel a great deal of healing energy, so why wouldn't they be popular! Most empaths I know have no trouble attracting romantic relationships, their real problem lies in maintaining them and feeling comfortable exchanging energies with someone day, after day, after day, and being expected to continue to do so for an indefinite period. Sometimes in relationships the nicest words an empath will hear are "I'm just off out, see you later."

However much an empath might adore the partner in question, they somehow can't help but breathe a sigh of relief, knowing they'll finally get to spread their energy out, clear it thoroughly, and stop absorbing for a while! Absorbing their partner's thoughts about the day ahead, the stresses they might be experiencing at work, any pain or worries they might be experiencing, harmless thoughts about what they might want to have for dinner, and who's going to cook it for them! Thoughts about what they might do at the weekend and how they felt when the new guy at work said that thing they said yesterday, and how they wish they'd dealt with it differently, and why haven't they had a pay-rise or been promoted, and are they any good at their job anyway, and does everyone know they're not, and on, and on …and on. Sometimes being in a relationship feels lovely to an empath, particularly with their intense ability to feel love, but sometimes, for an empath, the nicest thing about being with someone is finally being away from them for a while!

Because of this constant desire to detach, empaths respond very badly to partners who are possessive or who try to contain or restrict them in any way. Empaths will feel the toxicity of possessiveness in their bones, even before they spot any obviously possessive behaviour.

✓ **Empath Self-Care Tip:**

It is essential for empaths to spend a lot of time getting to know any potential partners before becoming intimate with them. There are a number of reasons why, once involved in a physically intimate relationship with a toxic partner, empaths will find it extremely difficult to disengage, and it could be years, or in some cases decades before an empath will finally detach from a possessive and controlling partner, once and for all. Many empaths, once attached and committed, would rather continue to believe that a toxic relationship can somehow be miraculously healed and fixed than face the pain of becoming psychically, emotionally and energetically detached from someone they have become addicted to.

○ **Too much interaction with anyone**

It's not only excessive time spent with intimate partners that can pull empaths into a state of despondency and overwhelm. Even the most saintly, easy-going and low-stress, low-maintenance friend or companion can set an empath's nerves on edge if too much time is spent in their company with not enough time and space allocated to simply staring into space and decompressing.

Here's a brief illustration of a phenomenon I have experienced countless times when flat sharing, even with the nicest, loveliest of people.

It's evening, I've just finished work teaching or giving readings online. I listen carefully at the door for a while until everything becomes quiet, knowing I've been working all day and will need time to process a *lot* of different energies before I'll be ready for even light-hearted conversation. I'm extremely hungry and looking forward to a nice solitary snack, back in my room.

Convinced there's no one else around, I make a dash for the kitchen, where I begin to hastily pull together a cold snack (cooking takes too long and could easily get me trapped). I'm planning to return to my room as soon as the peanut butter is spread and the bananas are peeled, knowing I need at least an hour of scrummy peace and quiet after all the intensity of the day's energy-exchanges.

On the other side of the door, the person I'm staying with has also been listening out for signs of movement, only with completely reversed intent, and somehow, within seconds of my arrival in the kitchen, they stealthily emerge from their room like a ninja, and I suddenly find myself in the middle of a full-blown conversation about how awful their day was!! Coincidence....?! And that, my friends, almost sums up the entire dynamic of why empaths need to avoid excessive interaction and why it's sometimes harder than you think.

✓ **Empath Self-Care Tip:**

As much as possible, weave little time and space treats and structures into your day and build them into your life. For example, wake up earlier than everyone else and grab an extra hour of alone time for breakfast. Keep a kettle and mini-fridge in your room or office – not so you can become a hermit or be completely antisocial, but simply to create extra decompression time when needed. If you work from home, give yourself a specific lunch hour and try to get out to a park or into a garden during that time – if possible, make sure it's a time when no one else is going to be around, especially if your work already involves using a lot of psychic energy and you need to remain clear and in balance.

o **Clutter and Dirt**

Everything carries a vibration, and many empaths who aren't even aware of this, or who wouldn't necessarily describe things in those terms, are sensitive to the vibrational emanations of dirt, chaos and clutter. Even many non-empaths will shudder involuntarily when confronted with a dirty bathroom or a pile of unwashed clothes strewn randomly across a floor. There's something almost visceral about the most common human response to dirt and clutter, and it's no surprise that so many of us respond well to in a clean, well-ordered space containing fewer items to engage with. Perhaps this is one of the many reasons for the popularity of de-cluttering books and TV programs.

Clutter and hoarding carry a low vibrational frequency and, as many of us are now raising our vibration, we are perhaps becoming less tolerant of mess and chaos. For empaths, clutter is at best distracting and at worst debilitating. There's just too much distraction, too much visual chatter and too many things pulling on our energy. This isn't to say that all empaths are pristinely tidy housekeepers and obsessive clean freaks, not at all. There are times when a little bit of creative chaos is necessary while we focus on more important things, but you won't find many empaths who are hoarders or who stuff their homes with things because they're of sentimental or any other kind of value. What most empaths value above all else, is peace, and to most empaths, a beautiful, serene, unencumbered, space – of a mental, emotional or physical nature - beings peace, sweet, perfect peace.

Many psychic empaths are extremely sensitive to the low frequencies given off by dirt, and when this happens, it is very unpleasant. As beautiful and powerful as it is to commune with the energies of crystals, trees, rivers and essential oils, it can be equally unpleasant to feel the vibrations of dirt. On the positive side, because empaths are so good at feeling and sensing these energies, they make excellent space-clearers and Feng Shui practitioners because they have an uncanny knack of knowing how to move and clean the energy in a room and feeling when the job is done.

✓ **Empath Self-Care Tips:**

Close your eyes and sense the energy in your home. See if there are any rooms or areas you feel drawn to. If you feel depressed, angry or uncomfortable in your home for no reason, ask your higher self and your energy radar to guide you to the places and spaces that most need clearing. Use, sage to smudge, or burn essential oils and play sacred music throughout the house. Open the windows and let some fresh air in.

One of the most powerful and perhaps most underrated ways to clear the energy in your home is to simply have a good clean, from top to bottom if possible. Use essential oils, Florida water, sea salt and baking soda in the water when you mop the floor and wipe the surfaces, burn essential oils in a burner and play sacred music as you work your way through the spaces. Keep going until you can feel the fresh uplifting lightness all around you, and keep things as clean and tidy as possible, on a day-to-day basis.

o **Noise**

Most empaths and sensitive people are very deeply affected by noise. Unexpected, unwanted or prolonged noise can feel like another form of attack on the energy field of the empath. In fact, any form of intrusion can feel oppressive for empaths and sensitives alike. For a sensitive person, the noise will feel like an assault on the senses, but an empaths will also absorb any extreme emotion associated with the noise. A psychic empath might suddenly be alerted to the crises involved on hearing ambulance sirens blaring. Psychically, they may visit the scene of the accident and immediately feel the pain of those involved.

Even when there is beautiful music playing, empaths need to have their aural rights respected. For example, an empath who lives with a musician who is in the habit of practicing their instrument from morning till night, can be driven to a state of depression and high anxiety. The unrelenting sound and repetition of the music, however beautiful it might sound to others, will be close to torture for the empath, who has now not only lost another safe recovery space, but who is also forced to absorb the consciousness of the musician during every waking hour, as it travels into their ears and psyche with each vibrating string.

The ups and downs of temperament, the insecurities and fragilities and any narcissistic tendencies that might be plaguing them in their fantasies about being able to someday make the grade. With every strum of the guitar or plonking of the keys, the empath's sensitive vibratory field is strummed into submission until life becomes unbearable.

We are all essentially vibrational beings, and empaths are like the tuning forks of the cosmos. We are here to set a pleasing tone that will create harmony between everything, but when people want to play out of tune, sometimes we're forced to vibrate right along with whatever else is being played.

✓ **Empath Self-Care Tips:**

Switch off the TV and mainstream radio as much as possible and choose which sounds you let in. Enrich your mind by filling your ears with podcasts on positive and inspirational topics or educating yourself on a favourite subject or hobby.

Give yourself regular periods of complete silence. This might sometimes mean even avoiding the positive, motivational input for a while, in order to enjoy spending time alone with your own thoughts.

As much as possible, when choosing which kind of music to listen to or selecting any other kind of input, pay special attention to the way it makes you feel, and opt for music and other input that brings you peace and joy.

Keep away from naturally noisy people and places.

○ **Arguments, Raised Voices and any Kind of Violence**

Similar to noise, arguments, loud voices and all forms of violence are absorbed by empaths and can feel like a personal attack, even when they're not directed specifically towards them.

When people are speaking in raised voices or arguing within earshot of an empath, their violent intentions can be felt and experienced as little daggers and darts penetrating the energy field and chakras of the empath. There may even be times when an aggressive person raises their voice at an empath and even though the sound might not seem as loud or as angry to others as it feels to an empath, nevertheless, the violence penetrates deeply. This is because empaths will feel the vibration of the anger ringing through them and vibrating in their ears during the attack, and long after it has ended.

✓ **Empath Self-Care Tip:**

Stay away from angry, violent and argumentative People!

○ **Dogmatic People and Controlling Behaviour**

When the people around an empath are excessively opinionated, arrogant, dogmatic or controlling, the empath can quickly begin to feel confined and oppressed. A controlling person may believe their behaviour has gone unnoticed and that the empath is naïve and easy to dominate or manipulate, but what they don't realise is that most empaths are only too well aware of their tricks, and could probably predict their next move before they even think of it! The problem is that when someone the empath is engaging with has a very strong agenda, an empath can sometimes experience this as a sharp pulling sensation in their solar plexus. So, when faced with a very controlling and dogmatic person, an empath will sometimes submit to their requests simply to keep the peace and to return to a state of painlessness.

Empaths know deep down how immature these people are but still sometimes genuinely believe they might be able to help heal them in some way. But generally, it never works out this way and empaths who allow toxic people to remain in their lives or who spend too much time in their company, will inevitably end up feeling suffocated, resentful, used and debilitated.

✓ **Empath Self-Care Tip:**

Begin to release toxic people from your life or spend as little time with them as possible! There's no way you can fix everyone and, in many cases, the underlying emotional problems that cause controlling people to behave in selfish and narcissistic ways, cannot even be healed by a qualified therapist. Don't be a hero. Value your time and energy enough to banish these relationships from your life, so that you can be there for those who know how to love, honour and cherish you and your kind nature. Without judgement, allow these people to drift away peacefully as you turn your face towards goodness.

o **Feeling Rushed**

As we explored earlier, empaths need plenty of time, space and opportunities to breathe, decompress, re-energise and move through daily tasks mindfully. If we feel rushed or experience a lack of the necessary time to process disruptive energies and other kinds of unhealthy stimuli, we can easily become more overwhelmed and out of balance.

✓ **Empath Self-care Tip:**

Give yourself plenty of time to get ready for work and cultivate a habit of arriving at appointments early. It's much better to be too early and sit reading calmly while you wait, than to panic and end up taking the underground, getting trapped in a lift with a vampire or generally arriving in a stressed-out panic! Give yourself plenty of time to breathe through your day and be mindful. The more time you have, the less overwhelmed and vulnerable you will become and the easier it will be to clear out those toxic energies as you go through the day, rather than allowing them to accumulate intolerably.

o **Office Jobs and Controlling Work Environments**

Most of us spend a huge proportion of our waking lives at work, and because of the sheer volume of contact time involved, excessively structured, highly peopled and horribly confining work environments can be highly toxic for an empath. Empaths can become extremely triggered by losing their sense of space, freedom and choice. And being forced to spend hour after hour, day after day, week after week in a relatively small office space with a huge range personality types and energy profiles, can feel particularly stressful. This problem can be exacerbated if the empath's desk has been chosen for them and they happen to be positioned next to an energy vampire or someone else with a toxic agenda.

Jobs that dictate and predetermine an empath's every movement throughout the day, according to strict timetables and regimes, and which involve a great deal of inter-colleague socialising, are also terrible for empaths, as they leave little or no time for withdrawal, reflection and recharging. Most empaths I know are desperate to take their lunch breaks alone and quickly become freaked out on long training days, when there seems to be no escaping the dreaded inter-colleague group lunches and team-building tea breaks, without seeming like a complete and utter misfit.

✓ **Empath Self-Care Tips:**

Think of ways to improve your working life by carefully considering what you know about yourself and your needs, before making future career decisions. Don't be afraid to be very specific when journaling to get clear about your dream job. As empaths are so easily influenced by the opinions and thoughts of others, it's important to begin your job search, knowing exactly what you want and deciding that you won't change your mind or compromise, no matter what!

How many people do you want to work with? Do you want a job that gives you longer lunch breaks or one that relies more on working alone than on working in groups? Do you want to be office-bound, home-based or mobile? If you haven't already done so, do you want to start a whole new career, one which enables you to use your incredible spiritual and creative gifts? How can you incorporate more self-care into your workday schedule?

Sit down in a quiet meditative space and take some time to think it all through and write it all down. Answer the questions above if you think they might help to guide you, and jot down any further points that might occur to you along the way, about how to make your current job more pleasant. Can you schedule in a longer lunchbreak and work slightly later? Is it possible to forgo a long summer holiday and scatter your days off throughout the year, as special empath mental health days? Can you keep a few protective crystals in your desk drawer, or could you even place them on top of your desk without risking ridicule?

Give yourself the luxury of creating a work environment that works for you, regardless of what might (or might not) make sense to everyone else.

Empaths and Issues with Weight-Gain

There are many reasons why some empaths have issues with over-eating and weight-gain. Many sensitive people who habitually become overwhelmed by energetic and sensory overload might at some point during any given day find that the huge build-up of toxicity has become too immense for them to process. In the case of empaths, this energetic burden may feel even more intense, because empaths are natural energy sponges.

Empaths are the psychic cleansers of the cosmos; they are like millions of little organic vacuum cleaners, sucking up all the anger, pain and sadness of the world. So, not only are they easily overwhelmed by external stimuli, they are sometimes also overwhelmed by suddenly being confronted with more negative emotions than they can handle clearing at any given time – emotions which don't even belong to them but which can, nevertheless, swoop in at a moment's notice and threaten to overtake them.

Most empaths feel a desperate longing to escape from these feelings of overwhelm, and from the general weight of extreme sensation. Some turn to alcohol, drugs and other intoxicants, in an attempt to deaden the impact of these energies on their vibratory field and nervous system. While many others, knowing that they are far too sensitive to handle these substances, turn to food, and in particular, fatty, sugary foods, in an attempt to comfort and soothe themselves.

Some empaths also have an unconscious belief that if they carry extra padding on their bodies, they will become better able to cope with the onslaught of negative energies descending on them from the maelstrom of toxic vibrations swimming around in the outer world. For some empaths, the extra weight feels like a comforting blanket that keeps out some of the unwanted energies or slows down their penetration into the energy field.

Whatever the reasons for turning to food, many empaths have a unique relationship with sugar, fats and other kinds comfort food, and need to find healthier ways to deal with the energy imbalances they face. Otherwise, the ensuing weight issues can lead to an ever-perpetuating cycle of self-loathing, which in turn triggers even more comfort eating. I have seen this cycle many times in toxic relationships with narcissists and energy vampires. In these situations, when an empath is under daily psychic assault they often come to believe that there is no physical escape from their situation, and that the only escape route is through the cupboard door, and into the land of cookies, cakes and sweeties. I'm sad to say that I have personally experienced this utter desperation and this cupboard-love lifestyle, but I'm happy to say that I managed to pull myself back from the brink before the problem became a serious health issue. And you can too!

Don't get me wrong, I do still have the occasional treat, but I now view processed sugars, chocolate, cakes and similar foods as a highly addictive drug, so I monitor their effect on me very carefully, and check myself back into the lemon water lifestyle rehab if I notice myself slipping back into old habits!

These foods have little or no significant nutritional value, no, not even "healthy" dark chocolate (of which I would eat sometimes 200 grams in one sitting, at my lowest point, telling myself I probably needed the magnesium!!! – It's interesting to note that at no point did I ever seem to crave magnesium drops or magnesium supplements).

Below are some of the tips I used to pull myself out of this cycle.

✓ **Empath Self-Care Tips:**

Develop a passion for savoury food. Spend three days eating only savoury food, allowing only green apples for sweetness and see how quickly your tastes can change.

Squirt lemon juice over everything – lemon juice can help to reduce sugar cravings and who knows, you might even learn to love the taste! Drink lemon-water first thing in the morning to set the tone for the day ahead.

Remember that for recovering alcoholics there's no such thing as one drink. They know that, that one drink will lead to another, and another, and another, so they simply *must* abstain completely or risk becoming addicted again. So, if, for alcoholics, there's no such thing as one drink, then for empaths, there's no such thing as one cake, chocolate bar, ice-cream or sweetie.

Find other ways to comfort yourself and learn to see food as fuel rather than a way to stuff down unpleasant feelings.

Strike food off the list of things you use to celebrate, commiserate or reward yourself. When you have something to celebrate or commiserate, buy yourself some flowers, scented soap, lotion or bubble bath instead of chocolate, cookie dough or ice-cream. From now on, the only butter in your house should be Shea butter!

Spend time with healthy people who have a healthier, non-addictive approach to food and nutrition. Watch, learn and use those beautiful empathy skills to absorb the kind of consciousness that makes you crave good nutrition much more than you crave comfort food.

Find hobbies you feel passionate about, and that keep you too occupied to think about food.

Take up a hobby that generates happy chemicals in your brain and which allows you to shake off negative energy quickly – learn to cha cha cha, Charleston, lindyhop or samba.

Do as many things as you can to have fun without food, and find fun people to do them with.

- *Note: I am not a qualified dietitian and nothing in this book constitutes medical or dietary advice. These are simply things that worked for me. Please ensure you have no allergies and that there are no contraindications to your making use of these tips and suggestions.*

Self-Care for Empaths

At the very end of this book, you'll find an 'at-a-glance, quick-view list of some of the empath self-care tips I've shared with you throughout the book. I've included this list, so that you can see them all together when you're looking for inspiration, without needing to go back and read through each individual chapter to find them. When read together, they should add up to nothing short of an empath's self-care handbook. However, in this chapter I'll go into greater detail about the vast range of other essential, practical, day-to day self-care tips, which have kept me sane in recent decades.

So, what do we mean by self-care? Well, by now we know a lot about empaths, their unique needs and some of the considerations they need to make at work, in social situations and in relationships of all kinds. But what are some of the things empaths need to do on a regular basis, in order to take better care of themselves? Below are some of the categories for the areas and ways in which I believe most empaths need to administer generous self-care.

Emotional Self-care

○ **Learn to say 'no'**

Learning to say no is essential for empaths, and yet, sometimes they are absolutely the worst at doing this. Not only because we don't like to hurt anyone's feelings, but also because if we do, we will usually experience their disappointment. With time, patience and practice, you can learn to be more resilient when it comes to saying no, and use a few simple energy-clearing techniques to help you to resist the pull of toxic people who don't like to be told they can't always have what they want.

The first tool that might help you is a popular assertiveness technique in which you repeat one statement several times, until the insistent person finally accepts your response.

This technique is known in assertiveness training circles as the 'stuck record technique' because it involves the person who is working on becoming more assertive stating almost the same words or sentiment, repeatedly, like a stuck record. This is an excellent tool for setting limits and boundaries with energy vampires.

Here's an example: The phone rings and you answer it. As soon as you do, you remember that you'd decided to limit the amount of time spent on the phone with Janice - a friend and co-worker who, for as long as you've known her, has been a chatty energy vampire, the kind who only every talks about how miserable her life is, yet never does anything to change it, and shows no interest in anything that's happening in your life.

You: Hi Janice, how are you? (sinking feeling)

Janice: Horrible!!! You'll never guess what John did today?!!!

You: (deeper sinking feeling) what?

Janice: He made me stay behind for A WHOLE HOUR to finish writing Deborah's reports. You know, the ones she was supposed to have handed in LAST FRIDAY!!!! UNBELIEVEABLE! I mean how long have I been working there? She's been there five minutes and suddenly everyone's having to clean up after her, well I'm not having...

You: Ugh!! Sounds awful! (deeper and deeper, but somehow rallying) Janice, I'm really sorry, I just remembered, I wasn't really supposed to answer the phone, we were just about to go out to the cinema.

Janice: Oh great! Do you mind if I tag along? I could do with some light relief, and we could have a nice catch up face-to-face on the way there.

You: (Breathing deeply) Sorry Janice but it's the first time in ages we've had a date night and we were looking forward to just chilling out together. Let's catch up next week.

Janice: Oh. Okay, well I could always just come along and be really quiet. I promise, I won't talk about all this stuff, I really could just do with getting out for some fresh air.

You: Oh, what a shame you caught me at such a bad time. We were just about to get out and have our first date night in ages. We're really looking forward to just chilling out together.

Janice: Oh right, well what about if I bring Max along, to even up the numbers? Then the guys can hang out together while we have a nice girly chat.

You: Yes, we must definitely do that some time, it's just such a shame that tonight we've planned this lovely date night, just the two of us, chilling out together at the cinema.

It might seem a bit tricky to master at first, and you might even imagine that your responses will sound horribly repetitive to your friend. But you'd be surprised to discover how little of what we say is actually taken in by energy vampires. A lot of the time they're just listening to themselves and their own thoughts, or hastily trying to work out the next persuasion technique, desperate to get their vital supplies of delicious empath energy. Have a few goes at practicing this technique and know that it's absolutely okay for you to just say NO! Just because you want to!

After you've ended a conversation of this sort, you might have all kinds of guilty feelings and energy attachments, sent unconsciously by the person in question. This is the perfect time to do the grounding, energy-clearing and protection exercises below, to separate yourself from any chords, attachments and overshadowing you might have picked as a result of any attempted psychic manipulation.

You will get better at this exercise with practice. There's no need for your empathy to be a cause of eternal suffering. See it as an opportunity to learn more about the subtle vibrational world of these energy dynamics. Decide today that you will become an energy master, and that you will one day use your precious gifts to support those who will genuinely benefit from them, rather than those who just want to use you as an energetic dumping ground.

You might have also noticed that in this exercise, you were not being asked to become angry, raise your voice or do anything at all that would inspire conflict or strife among normal, well-balanced, kind and compassionate people like yourself. If the tables were turned, you would probably have accepted your friend's very first refusal, and this is one of the many things that makes you so loveable - your understanding and your ability to immediately see things from another person's point of view. So, don't you deserve the same kind of treatment from your friends?! Just something to ponder...

o   **Ask for What You Want and Be Specific**

Learn how to ask for what you want rather than simply going along with whatever presents itself to you. If you'd feel better going out for a walk by the sea, try asking for that rather than allowing yourself to get dragged along to pub quiz after pub quiz. Your true friends will be more understanding than you might think.

When you journal about what you want to create or manifest, be specific with the universe and ask for *exactly* what you want. Remember, many of the things we call manifestations, are plans, things we intend to execute on rather than things we're waiting for the universe to deliver. So be specific. What qualities are you looking for in a mate? What sort of area do you want (or need) to live in, where, how, when and with whom do you want to work? How do you want your life to look five years from now in order to be the most comfortable and safe, while also fulfilling the divine purpose for which you came to Earth? Once again, be extremely specific, don't just say you want to be a healer: do you want to work one to one, with small groups or start a centre for other healers? Or do you want to teach other healers but not have personal clients? Would you prefer to work from home of work in a clinic? How many years/months/weeks do you want to train? What size group do you want to train in? Where do you want to do your training? What needs to change in order for life to support you in being the brightest and best version of yourself?

Keep a Sense of Humour

As an empath, you may read this book and think, what a gloomy business it is being an empath! There must be some very dull and miserable ones out there! However, I know that as an empath, your ability to feel things very deeply includes the ability to feel very positive, happy, high vibrational feelings as well. And I haven't forgotten for a moment that, because of their deeply incisive and detailed observation abilities empaths can be hilariously funny! We're simply going into greater depth over the areas I feel you might need the most help with.

I know that on the right sort of night, in the right sort of company, many of the empaths reading this book will be out having a complete hoot, watching some great comedy show, hopefully with equally fun friends! And this is another essential aspect of empath self-care. There's nothing like a good laugh for putting things back into perspective, and laughter also has a very light and high vibration. Most empaths I know love to laugh, and when they do the sound vibration of their laughter will ripple through their energy field like wind chimes, breaking up stagnant energy, releasing anxiety, cleansing, clearing and raising their vibration and producing a variety of feel-good chemicals and hormones in the brain.

Try not to let those unpleasant and overwhelming feelings get to you. Get out there and have some fun. Learn to laugh it off sometimes.

o **Limit the Amount of World News You Read or Watch on TV:**

In fact, limit or remove TV from your life completely if you can. Most television news, and even some commercials, television programs and films are packed with unpleasant images and seem to emit a constant steam of low-level fear and anxiety. As an empath, you don't need to be assaulted by these energies or by emotional scenes and stories of disasters, violent crimes, poverty and starvation. Keep your vibration high, so that one day, you can contribute something to the world instead.

Indulging in conversations and drama about how terrible things are, will only make you feel terrible, and all those sad stories will only make you feel depressed and hopeless. If you're concerned about the images you might suddenly be subjected to while watching a new film, or a more violent/creepy 'remake' of a film that was only made a few years ago, don't be embarrassed to go and find the original somewhere and re-watch that instead.

Immerse yourself in pleasant, happy-go-lucky films with nice and fun, predictable events and storylines. Just one tiny, unexpected image can trigger most of us for days, so go ahead and recycle those old Eddy Murphy films, or get out some classic, old school Tom Hanks/Meg Ryan romantic comedies.

Physical Self-Care

o **Work on Your Physical Health and Fitness**

Get enough sleep and take naps whenever you need to, without self-judgement.

Eat healthy, life-giving, nutritious foods and stay away from harmful chemicals and intoxicants wherever possible. Value your precious nervous system and be kind to your body in every, possible way. No one's perfect and there may still be times when the overwhelm feels too strong to be dealt with in healthy ways but do the best you can to establish a healthy norm in your overall daily routines and lifestyle.

o **Get out More**

Yep, I said it! As tempting as it can be to stay at home and cosy up on the sofa at every available opportunity, protracted periods spent indoors will only weaken your 'outdoors' muscles and make it harder for you to force yourself out when you need to. Have you ever noticed how hard it can sometimes feel to face the outside world after an entire weekend spent in reclusive hibernation?! Even if you don't live in the countryside or by the sea, there will always be a bus service that travels virtually from your front door to somewhere else that feels like a fresh, new experience. Keep this muscle exercised and maintain contact with the outside world. There are so many fun things you could be missing out on if you continue to hide away. Move your body, go for long walks, stay fit and healthy and resist the temptation to cuddle up on the sofa with hot chocolate and cakes. Cake is not your friend!

Practice using the techniques in this book and experiment with venturing a little further outside your comfort zone each week. No matter what you've been through, never stop believing that the world can still surprise you in wonderful and unexpected ways. Your tribe could be waiting for you at the end of the next bus ride.

o **Physically Remove Yourself from Sources of Emotional Disturbance**

Practice getting used to the idea that it's okay for you excuse yourself from people, places and situations you find uncomfortable. If someone corners you at a dinner party, in a supermarket queue or in any other situation, it's perfectly fine for you to move away to another room, place-setting or queue. Even if it feels extremely rude to do this, no one would object to your excusing yourself to go to the bathroom or running off to grab the quinoa that you seem to have forgotten. Once there, you can either practice some deep breathing and energy-clearing techniques or plan your exit properly. Don't feel you have to endure situations that feel toxic.

Mental Health Self-Care

o **Stay Away from Drama**

Avoid personal drama and over thinking and try to also avoid engaging in drama in the way you speak to others, the things you listen to, the gossip and information you pass on and recycle. The energy of these things has a very low frequency, and even despite the almost irresistible temptation to dwell on personal slights and upsets when we're feeling hurt or betrayed, replaying these things in your mind, burdening others with them or turning them over from every angle with anyone, anywhere online who will listen, will only keep you stuck in the lower energy that created the drama.

Learn to pick yourself up, dust yourself off and start all over again as quickly as possible. Try not to hold grudges or take these stresses and attacks with you into the dream state at night. Let it all go, using any of the energy-clearing techniques I'll share with you later in the book, and use the time and mental space you create, to learn a new skill or make something beautiful instead.

o **Unplug!**

Treat yourself to a technology and communications holiday from time to time, and take complete breaks from being reachable online, via email, social media or even texts and phone calls. Many years ago, before the appearance of smart phones and social media, it was much easier for empaths, and everyone else, to find time and space to simply be alone with their thoughts and connect with something far greater, wiser and more peaceful. Many of us took it for granted that we were able to go for several hours without checking a phone or checking in with anyone about anything at all. We were free to simply be.

In today's fast-moving, ever-encroaching technological age, it's sometimes impossible to find time to simply sit still and breathe. Mental health issues among the world's wealthiest nations are on the increase and suicides have reached record levels. Something must be done!

Dear empath, if you even begin to suspect that you are reaching technological overwhelm, try this simple technology detox and see what benefits it brings, perhaps in the form of an increased sense of peace, stability and mental presence. Tell your friends you'll be limiting your use of technology for a few days, in order to rest and recharge. Then totally indulge yourself in the blissful peace and quiet that will follow.

Take a whole day off and go for restorative walks or sit quietly for an hour, doing nothing more than listen to yourself thinking and breathing. Read books made of paper. Smell their pages and turn them slowly, mindfully and indulgently. Gaze at the sunset and make a long, lingering dinner before sinking into a sumptuous, silent bubble bath, or just listing to some gentle music and watching the trees swaying in the wind. Welcome to the real world, Neo. Enjoy!

Environmental Self-Care

o **De-Clutter Your Home**

De-clutter your surroundings and reduce the number of objects and distractions pulling on your attention and energy.

o **Evaluate Your Surroundings**

Consider the places you regularly spend time. Are they healthy? Is your working environment a place that supports you or one that drains you? Is your journey to work inspiring and uplifting or does it suck all the life out of you before you've even arrived?

Spiritual and Energetic Self-care

o **Separate Yourself from Others and Clear Your Energy**

As much as possible, separate your feelings from the feelings of those around you. If you feel full of the joys of spring one minute, and the next you feel overshadowed, downcast or depressed, you will have almost certainly absorbed energy that belongs to someone else.

Spend time each day asking yourself, does this energy truly belong to me? Is it really mine? If the answer is no, try to find a quiet place to sit still, breathe and practice the following exercise:

Energy Separation Exercise

Close your eyes and, using your intuition and clairsentience, search your body for the energetic invasion, until you find the place where you feel the negative energy sitting.

As soon as you connect with the energy, simply say these words:

I call the divine with love and light, to dissolve this negativity from my solar plexus (or whichever words apply) **and to fill the spaces with divine love. Thank you! And so it is.**

Wait a few minutes or until you feel the energy shifting. Then take a few deep breaths, and with each incoming breath, mentally set your intention to fill your entire body with even more of this protective and supportive light.

o   **Begin a Daily Meditate Meditation Practice**

The benefits of meditation have been widely documented and its ability to generate peaceful and productive states of mind have led to its use in schools, hospitals, prisons, workplaces and in many other settings where peace and balance are greatly valued.

Meditation increases memory, creativity, compassion, concentration, cell renewal, optimism and emotional regulation. So, it's no wonder that we have seen such a vast and rapid increase in its popularity over the last few decades.

As an empath, it is essential that you take time every day to connect with yourself. This will allow you to gradually develop a greater awareness of where your energy exists in time and space and what its qualities feel like. This way, it will become progressively easier for you to notice whether a foreign or unwanted energy has entered your aura, so that you can clear it quickly, and return to peace and balance.

As an empath, some of your meditations will need to have a more psychic flavour to them, as any progress that you make in developing your psychic and intuitive gifts will increase your ability to discern the different qualities of energy existing throughout the cosmos, and to clear them when you experience psychic intrusion.

Meditation can also enable empaths to connect with their feelings and get to know themselves better. When living with people who have strong agendas, or engaging with them on a daily basis, you might find it necessary to do conduct daily energy-clearing and separation exercises, as a vital part of your meditations. Getting to know yourself better, emotionally and energetically, will enable you to know when any mental confusions have been brought on by overshadowing. Daily meditation will increase your ability to discern what your true desires are, and which ones are being imposed on you from external sources.

This might all sound like a lot of work, but I promise you it will be worth every drop of effort you put in. So, do whatever you need to do, with quiet equanimity, and continue to view yourself as a master-in-training. See your empathy as the greatest psychic development school ever created, and your feelings of resentment will soon dissipate or dissolve into fascination! One day, you will give thanks for these gifts, and a daily meditation practice, accompanied by studious journaling about what you discover in these sessions will enable you to know your own mind and do what you came here to do.

Daily meditation could be everything you need to clear up any confusion you currently have about your soul development, personal choices, life purpose and career path.

o   **Become More Selective about Physical Contact**

Remember that every time you hug or embrace someone or allow them to spend time in close proximity, you are exchanging energy with them. Before you hug, kiss or become physically intimate with someone, ask yourself this question:

"Would I be happy to become this person or to become very similar to them?"

You know that as an empath, you are more than likely to absorb not only the feelings, but also the consciousness of the people you allow to get physically close to you and remain in your energy-field for prolonged periods of time.

Those empaths who have experienced relationships with narcissists will know exactly what I mean. How long after returning from a rejuvenating weekend away with some lovely, inspiring people, did it take for you to find yourself back in the narcissist's mindset, when you found yourself back in his or her company? How long after those first sweet, tentative reunion hugs, kisses and shenanigans did you find yourself feeling heavy, cynical, gossipy and disgruntled?

Remember, hugs, kisses and intimacy are always a choice. Guard those treasures carefully. Energy is transferred very quickly through touch, and even through sustained eye-contact. Have you ever noticed how energy vampires and narcissists like to insist on capturing your complete attention? How many times have you heard the words: "You're not listening are you?!?!???" even when they're not saying anything particularly earth-shattering or interesting. Purely on instinct, you have been carefully avoiding excessive contact with their deadly gaze, because you know on some level that giving them too much attention will allow them to drain you. Unfortunately, they also know that giving them your full attention will allow them to drain you.

○ **Develop Good Conversational Boundaries**

If you're uncomfortable with someone you've just met, try to resist being drawn into deep and intense conversations with them, particularly as you don't know them very well. Try to keep dinner party conversation light and breezy, especially when meeting people for the first time, and, when in doubt, discreetly limit eye contact and physical touch. Have you ever noticed how strangers will sometimes want to keep touching your arm when they're speaking to you? Doesn't this strike you as strange behaviour from someone you've just met? Empaths are social catnip for energy vampires and they will employ some very clever and unexpected tricks to open you up and suck you dry if you let them.

Try to refrain from discussing psychic and metaphysical topics in inappropriate contexts – the conversation and your own enthusiasm for the subject may be used to drain you. Whenever we discuss matters of a spiritual nature, whether we are aware of it or not, we begin to open up our energy-centres, just as we might open up before doing any kind of spiritual work. This can leave us open to all kinds of unwanted influences and make us even more vulnerable to energy-draining people. So, there you are, having a seemingly innocent pub conversation about how much you love crystals and Reiki, with your energy-field all lit up like a Christmas tree, and suddenly, there's an energy vampire standing beside you, appearing as if from out of nowhere.

Oh, says he or she, *I've heard a lot about that sort of thing, don't believe a word of it!* And there you are, lovely, kind, spiritual, caring, sharing lightworker you, triggered as heck and wondering whether to take the bait and jump in with endless facts and figures about scientific studies conducted on a group of people with Alzheimer's, and the undeniable results. But then you suddenly remember what you've read here in this kindly book of seasoned-empath wisdom, and you quietly back off and retreat to the bathroom to clear, shield and protect your energy. You have nothing to prove dear empath. Awaken and become the spiritual warrior your soul is calling you to be and you will soon be sharing your truths in lovely lecture halls filled with people who wish to hear, spread and share them.

Never be afraid to excuse yourself to go and "powder your nose" if things get too intense too soon. Even if you're wrong about the energy vampire you will have lost nothing. And at the end of the evening, your make-up will be immaculate, your energy will be clear and you'll probably be the most matt person in the room. You're welcome!

o **Make Use of the Magic of Water**

As well as being aware of its physical cleansing benefits, many empaths can also feel the life-giving, cleansing vibrations of water, particularly water which has been blessed or energised. If you're in any doubt about the immense power of water and haven't yet heard of Dr Masaru Emoto, please google that name and begin to make your daily bath or shower a deeply restorative energy-clearing ritual.

o **Spend Time in Nature**

This is one of the most powerful tools empaths can make use of. Most empaths are very in tune with nature and many can see, sense or feel the living, loving vibrations and energetic emanations that surround trees, flowers and moving bodies of water.

All of nature wishes to communicate with us and assist us in our ascension process, and in all our daily struggles. The trees, the sea and even the sun can act as powerful energy-clearing tools that will not only extract and neutralise negative energy but will also help us to ground and centre ourselves.

As often as possible, get out into nature and allow the trees, the flowers, the sunshine and the sea to cleanse and restore your depleted energy field.

○ **Spend Time Alone**

Find ways to occasionally be completely alone, without anyone else in your physical space and with no specific plans to meet anyone. Let yourself have an energy holiday in which there's no need to experience the constant stress and anxiety connected with processing all the energy in the room, including your own, and feeling exhausted just from making eye contact with a stranger.

○ **Get Grounded**

Learn how to get grounded when you feel thrown off balance. Grounding is an essential aspect of psychic and energetic protection.

In the next chapter we'll explore Grounding in more detail and I'll share some grounding techniques you might find useful.

Why Grounding is Essential for Empaths

Many people who are sensitive can quickly become very ungrounded after a psychic attack or as a result of any kind of extreme, negative, mental, emotional, physical or spiritual encounter. Without knowing it, many empaths will unconsciously attempt to leave their bodies, as a way of escaping the sudden energetic onslaught, but this can only serve to leave us even more vulnerable. Being spaced-out is never a pleasant way to feel as you wander through a crowded shopping centre feeling insulted and assaulted.

Being grounded can not only bring you greater presence of mind in handling these tricky situations, it can also help to keep the vital energy flowing in your body - the very energy you need to call in to defend yourself against these attacks. It may seem counter-intuitive to remain in a body that seems to just wander around absorbing pain all day, but I promise you that if you learn these vital grounding skills and techniques, you will gradually become stronger and more in control of your life.

So, what is grounding? Well grounding essentially is any practices, techniques, tools or rituals we use to re-centre ourselves, re-connect with the earth and attune ourselves to the more earthy qualities of our practical 3d reality, and this is why 'grounding' is also sometimes known as 'earthing.'

There are many ways to ground yourself and re-stablish a productive and responsible connection with your Earth reality, and each empath will find a different technique, tool or practice useful. You might find that different methods work better at different times or in different circumstances. Look at the list below and see which grounding techniques you're most drawn to. Make a start today and see what changes a powerful grounding technique can bring into your life.

Grounding Techniques and How to Use Them Effectively

- Walking barefoot on the earth or sand – Get outside and place your feet on the earth, somewhere it feels safe to do this. Sit quietly, breathe, and simply focus on connecting with the earth and receiving pure, unconditional love through the soles of your feet. Mother Gaia understands what you're going through and is willing to be your friend and ally in all your struggles

- Massaging your feet – Massaging your feet brings your attention, and therefore your energy, back into your body. Any kind of massage can be quite grounding but remember to only receive massage from people whose energy feels good to you

- Wearing crystals – Wearing certain crystals close to the body can help empaths to feel more grounded and connected to the earth. Experiment with crystals in red or brown shades and also wear some black stones such as black tourmaline: to shield and protect your energy from psychic intrusion, and shungite: to block psychic attacks from lower life forms, EMFs and harmful environmental radiations

- Using natural materials and fabrics in your home and clothing as much as possible, and filling your home with things of the earth – plants; crystals; shells; polished stones; pretty rocks; wooden objects, furniture and floorboards; cotton throws and bamboo furniture

- Using essential oils – There are a number of essential oils you can use to help ground yourself. One of my favourite things to do is massage my feet with Patchouli oil. It has often been said that in the 1960s when spiritual and psychic awakenings were happening at an unprecedented pace, one of the reasons Patchouli was so popular among hippes was because of its grounding abilities. Personally, I have found this one oil to be very powerful and effective for grounding, but feel free to experiment with other very earthy oils such as cedarwood, rosewood, benzoin and pine

- Connecting with nature in a physical way (tree hugging) – If possible, get out into a park, a forest or into the woods and find a huge tree to sit with. Tree-hugging can be a wonderful experience for empaths, as we can feel the love, friendship and protection of these beautiful, magnificent ancient beings. However, you might find that it's enough to simply sit on the ground or on a picnic blanket with your back to a tree, soaking up its loving vibrations and allowing its seniority, wisdom and rootedness to lovingly connect you to the earth

- Meditation with visualisation – This is one of the most powerful ways to become grounded, centred and balanced in any place, at any time. Read through the grounding and psychic protection meditations below, and practice them daily until they become more fluid and natural. The more you work with these techniques, the easier it will be for you to use them quickly when you slip away for a bathroom break, or to repair yourself after an encounter with an energy vampire

Grounding and Psychic Protection Meditations

These meditations can be life changing. In fact, many of my students have told me that their lives have improved beyond description after working with them for just a few weeks.

Take as much time as you need at each stage, making sure you feel the changes taking place, every step of the way. Each of these processes can take just a few minutes when you are more familiar with them; however, it's important never to rush through them, as the energies around us are constantly changing. In my experience, when they take a bit longer, it's always worth spending the extra time, simply for the wonderful effect they will have on your life and your overall energetic and physical health.

Grounding Meditation

Begin by seeing, feeling a huge and powerful ray of Divine White Light, pouring down from the heavens. See, sense feel or simply trust and imagine it steaming through the clouds and rushing in through the roof of your home and into your crown chakra, flowing down through your entire energy system until you are filled with this beautiful Divine Light, and a peaceful feeling of pure, eternal, unconditional love.

See, sense, feel or imagine this light expanding and becoming stronger, as it goes quickly streaming through you, filling each chakra, and your entire body, as it travels all the way down to your legs and feet, as well as through the root chakra.

Feel it travelling deep into the crystalline centre of the new Earth and anchoring you there fully and firmly. As the light travels down from your feet, imagine it pouring itself into the centre of the earth, as a series of giant roots of light, flowing down and grounding and rooting your entire being, connecting you in Divinity and sacredness, to the loving heart of Mother Earth.

At this stage, you might feel your feet tingling, or experience other kinds of shifts within your energy body. See these as a little sign that something powerful is taking place and that you are beginning to reconnect and earth yourself in a way that will bring you the peace, protection and balance you've been seeking. Breathe deeply into this feeling. Relax, let go, and allow the earth to carry you, to love you, to heal you, just as it was always meant to.

Stop and notice that somewhere in this Divine space at the heart of Mother Earth, there is a huge, ancient forest, full of enormous, ancient trees.

Find one tree that you feel particularly drawn to and allow your roots to connect with *its* roots and feel an immense wave of love and protection flowing towards you from this wise and loving, ancient tree person.

Take time to enjoy every step of this wonderfully relaxing and centring process. Stay here for a while enjoying the Divine Presence of Mother Earth. Don't rush; remember that gradually becoming accustomed to feeling grounded in this way is an important aspect of your development as an empath.

This may seem like a lot to take in on paper, but please feel free to record any of these techniques (purely for your own personal use) and listen back to them as you visualise, making sure to leave plenty of spaces in the recordings to really feel your way into the exercises.

Psychic Protection Meditation

There are three powerful forms of psychic protection that I usually teach my students to use once they have completed the grounding exercise.

The first level of protection is personal, the second is local and the third is environmental. Please see the detailed explanations below.

Once again, it's important to remember that even though it may take some time to perform these techniques when you're just getting started, once you get used to them, you'll find that it gets easier and the entire process becomes much quicker to perform. So, in the beginning, it's important to give yourself as much time as you need to set up the process properly. Go through each stage slowly and mindfully, making sure you feel the energy shifting and the protection growing, before moving on to the next stage.

1 Personal – Picture a large, deep blue velvet cloak, with electrical shimmers, and sparkles of gold, silver and blue light. This cloak is thick, comforting and filled with Divine Love and protection. Take a minute or two to observe its sparkles and shimmers, and notice that a large and magical being is holding this cloak and offering it to you. This being is Archangel Michael. See him with his mighty silver sword, glistening and glimmering, his silver breastplate also sparking and glinting magically.

Feel or imagine yourself reaching out to put one of your arms into this magical, electric blue shimmering cloak. Notice how it feels. Feel its loving, protective quality all around you, as you gratefully accept it and feel the entire cloak now being placed over your shoulders, the hood now covering your head. Feel how the energy changes, as Archangel Michael now zips this cloak all the way up to your chin. It is even being zipped up under your feet. And your sacred roots of Divine light are flowing through it and continuing to keep you grounded. Stay inside this cloak, with the hood gently covering and closing your third eye, keeping out all unwanted energies. Relax, breathe.

2 Local – The second protective symbol I like to use is one that also covers you, but which also covers the room or larger area you're sitting in. Imagine a large, golden pyramid or dome, coming down from heaven, carried by angels of love, light and ascension. See this heavy structure in detail. Notice its thick, heavy golden bricks as it slowly descends, completely covering you and most of the room you're sitting in. If it is a pyramid, see its corners touching the corners of your room, and as it lands on the ground, see a thick carpet of gold unrolling under your feet so that you're now completely encased within it, still wearing your beautiful, protective cloak, with your roots of light still flowing through into the earth and continuing to ground you.

With each of these protections, wait until you see or feel them taking shape around you, then take time to fully notice the energetic impact they have on you, and on the energetic atmosphere around you.

3 Environmental – The third and final protection in this sequence is petitioning the Band of Mercy. With your eyes still closed, ask Archangel Michael to surround you, the room you're sitting in, your home, and the surrounding area with his loving, protective angels, (without affecting the free will of anyone else nearby) and to charge them with keeping out all energies of a lower frequency. This enormous congregation of angels is often referred to as the Band of Mercy. They can be seen in many great paintings as hoards of angels with huge, white wings, all dressed in white robes, assembled in the sky or wherever they are needed.

Once you have petitioned protection from the Band of mercy, take time to sit quietly, simply feeling their love and protection, and sensing them shielding everything with their protective love and light.

I also suggest asking Archangel Michael to place a veil of camouflage over all of this vibrant light, so that it can only be seen by loving eyes. You can also ask Archangel Michael to stay with you as you go through your day, keeping you safe and protected against all unwanted energies.

Closing Down Psychically

One final psychic exercise that can help immensely with psychic protection, is to close and seal your chakras after completing psychic work or healing sessions and before going out in busy town areas, shopping centres and hypermarkets.

Note: This doesn't mean that we are shutting down our chakras or inhibiting their natural function in any way. It simply means, closing and shielding them against overwhelming and undesirable energies.

As you might already know from experience, open and unguarded auras and chakras can attract some very unproductive energies. Leaving your energy wide open is like keeping your front door open all day and all night, and then wondering why your home is full of strangers and kind of... empty.

Chakra Closing Exercise

Sit quietly and imagine the crown charka, sitting at the top of your head like a beautiful, giant lotus flower. Practice seeing, sensing or feeing whether this chakra is open, either fully or halfway, and ask the Divine light to very gently close and protect it against all unwanted energies. Visualise its petals closing gently and notice what you feel when this happens. Stay still and notice or intuit when it has closed fully and then move down to the 3rd eye chakra.

Picture each of the chakras as an open flower of an appropriate colour for the energy centre you're working on, and continue in this way until you have closed each chakra, one by one, taking time to feel and notice any energy changes, before moving on to the next one.

When you get to the root chakra, quickly check once again, that you are still grounded and connected to the earth and that the light from heaven is still connecting with you at the crown chakra.

Feel the Divine protective cloak or Archangel Michael enveloping you once again, and if anything about the closing down process is unclear, please ask Archangel Michael to make sure you are fully closed down. Sit quietly, noticing any changes as he works, and then slowly come back to earth and open your eyes.

Essential Oils for Empaths

There are several oils that will support you as an empath. These are just a few that you may find powerful for various spiritual or personal development purposes.

Use **Orange, Peppermint, Lemon, Rosemary and Lavender** oils in a burner, in your home or meditation space for general day-to-day space-clearing.

- **Orange** is very cheerful and uplifting and will disperse stagnant energies from arguments or unpleasant thoughts.

- **Peppermint** can help to ease depression, release entities and break up stagnant emotional patterns, and thought forms

- **Lavender** is great for all cleansing. It's like the violet flame in a bottle.

- **Lemon** and **Rosemary** are both wonderful spiritual cleansers

Once again, I would highly recommend massaging the feet with **Patchouli oil,** particularly on the soles of your feet, for grounding purposes.

If you wish to use your empathy to develop your psychic and spiritual gifts, massage **Bay** oil into the 3rd eye area for heightened perception.

You can also mix some **Orange, Peppermint** and **Lavender** with water in a spray bottle to use as an energy-clearing spray all around your home or workspace. Alternatively, you can mix it with carrier oil and keep it in a glass bottle. Rub it into the solar plexus area if you ever feel your energy is being compromised.

Add a few drops of **Peppermint, Lavender** and **Lemon Oils to some baking soda** or **Epsom Salts** in a glass container and shake the container until they are completely mixed. Use this mixture as a special energy-clearing bath salts mix to help release all the yucky energies you may have collected throughout the day.

- *Note: Please ensure you have no allergies and that there are no contraindications to your use of these very powerful oils and remember to always dilute them before use and to use them sparingly or under instruction.*

Why Empaths Attract Narcissists and How to Finally Break Free

There are many reasons why narcissists are attracted to empaths like moths to a flame. Perhaps one of the most powerful of these is the fact that narcissists are extremely wounded people ...and so are many empaths. Empaths feel the need to give, and give, and give in order to feel healed, and narcissists feel the need to take, and take, and take. So, in a sense, they make the perfect symbiotic, toxic partnership.

The reason I'm choosing to express the dynamic in this matter-of-fact way is not because I don't deeply sympathise with the empath; I am an empath myself, so of course I understand the dynamics from the empath position, entirely. I'm explaining the dynamics in those terms because I want to empower the empath to gently move beyond the tortured victim role, into a place where we can recognise precisely what it is that makes us want to endlessly give in this way, and begin fixing it.

Being a giver is a wonderful thing. It makes you a great healer, nurturer, therapist, lightworker, parent, practitioner and new age service provider. However, over-giving and giving inappropriately to people who will never be able to appreciate or truly benefit from what we give, is damaging for heart, mind, body, spirit and soul and, in the long term, it not only diminishes our lifeforce and dims our light, it also makes us unavailable to those who *would* benefit from our gifts.

While the world is waiting for you to step up in Divine service, one single malignant person is draining your lifeforce and keeping you stuck in a darkened room. Even if you manage to convince yourself that their brand of cruelty isn't *real* cruelty compared to what some people go through, is it really okay that you're not living your life at the highest expression of itself, or fulfilling your greatest potential? Is it really okay that your life has come to a standstill while so many people who need you don't even know you exist? It's time for you to end this pattern and move on.

Even though I know from personal experience how damaging these narcissistic relationships can be for an empath, I'm not going to dwell on this subject for too long. It has been covered extensively by a number of extremely well qualified, experienced and compassionate psychologists and psychotherapists. My plan for this section is to write something short and potent that will, hopefully, help to shake you out of your complacency and show you that, if you are still involved in one of these life-threatening connections, you are simply wasting your life away.

Dear empath, please find a way to break loose. I'm not saying this lightly. It took me several years to finally break free and I still occasionally wrestle in my mind with flashbacks to the very early love-bombing stage of the relationship, but I cannot tell you how much happier and more energised I am since I left.

There are an endless number of books, youtube channels and podcasts on the subject of narcissism, and I believe that it was these amazing resources that actually saved my life, and for that, I am eternally grateful.

In the end, it was actually a book that was not even explicitly about narcissists, which gave me the courage to finally move on with my life. Until I discovered that awesome and mighty book, I was completely and utterly addicted to the idea that one day, somehow, some way, the beautiful man I had fallen in love with nineteen years ago was going to return, and I would wake up to discover with utter relief, that it had all just been a bad dream. All the shouting episodes, the career sabotages, put downs, isolation from friends, exclusion from family weddings (even though we were living together at the time), the rejection on every level of my being, the unexplained coldness, the mood swings, the constant feeling of low-level displeasure, the frequent discards, the constant anxiety, the flying monkeys, the daily attempts to get me fat to hinder my career and to fill me with defeat and self-loathing, the sleepless nights when I would lie in bed thinking I was about to have a heart attack because of the most recent shouting episode and the general uncertainty of it all, the mind games, the gaslighting, the word salad, the fact that no one would believe me and there was no one I could talk to, and the maddening sense of betrayal by almost every single person in my life, who chose to believe him over me and left me feeling powerless, invalidated, lonely, despondent, suicidal and irrelevant, yes, I'm ashamed to say that despite all of this, I still thought he was going to change one day and that everything would be lovely-dovey and beautiful again.

Until I read the book that finally saved me. 'Dodging Energy Vampires' by Dr Christian Northrop. What this book made me realise is that that even if I could convince myself time after time, year after year, decade after decade, that these things were simply exaggerations of my mind, there was no way I could deny that being with this person constantly left me feeling completely and utterly, life-changingly exhausted and depleted, and that this was a big enough reason to let him go. It was that simple. The whole time I was convincing myself that he might not be actually being all *that* cruel, I was just talking myself back into staying. After all, no one else believed he could be that cruel, so why should I? There was literally NO ONE to validate my experience!!! But the book told me it didn't matter. I was drained, I felt bad every day, I wasn't happy, and that was enough! Thank you, Dr. N. You totally rock!!

Most empaths want to believe the very best of everyone and, so, believing that someone is irreparable is inconceivable to us. I used to tell myself that anything could be healed, and anyone could change if they were just given enough love. Well, that may well be true, but do you really want to spend the next twenty years finding out?

I'm not going to give you a handy list of tips to help you to understand your relationship better. You already understand it. You just haven't yet discovered that magical key that will finally unlock your prison door and allow you to set yourself free.

Put simply, even if you refuse to see that the emotional and mental abuse you have endured are very real, very damaging and extremely dangerous to your health. Even if you refuse to believe that the person in question is a truly cruel and vindictive person. Even if you're able to turn a blind eye to all the cruelty and injustices you have experienced within the relationship. Even if you're still convinced that your Mr Hyde is really the good-natured and kindly Dr. Jekyll and is just having a protracted bad day. Even if all of those delusions are keeping you convinced that nothing you see, sense feel, know and experience on a daily basis matters a hill of beans, the bottom line is quite simply this... Life is meant to be enjoyed, relationships should bring happiness into our lives, and if you're consistently unhappy and feel too drained to do things that *make* you happy, and this never ever changes, year after year ... that's a big enough reason to leave. RUN!!!!

Thank you for taking the time to read this book, dear empath. I hope it brings wonderful gifts of freedom, joy and renewed life to you.

Below, as promised, is the little section of quick-reference empath self-care tips. I hope you find them useful and refer to them daily, until everything falls into place for you.

Namaste

Empath Self-Care Tips at a Glance

✓ Fill your life with good people, good experiences and quality time all to yourself, and practice extreme self-care

✓ Take regular salt baths with essential oils, baking soda, Himalayan salt and/or Epsom salts

✓ Spend a lot of time getting to know any potential partners before becoming physically intimate with them

✓ Spend time pottering, mediating, reading and generally restoring yourself after clearing your energy. Set your expectation to live at a higher level of freedom, peace and joy, rather than simply existing in eternal fight or flight mode, careening from one energy-clearing emergency to the next

✓ Begin to release toxic people from your life or spend as little time with them as possible

✓ Before you go to sleep each night, take an energy inventory and release any stuck energy of anger, fear or sadness you may have picked up from others throughout the day. Try not to carry it with you through the night and into the next day. Release it and start again. Tomorrow is another day!

- ✓ Never, ever allow yourself to be rushed into a decision of any kind. You are absolutely entitled to say you need more time to think about an offer, and anyone pushing you to make a hasty decision in a very short space of time is a definite red flag

- ✓ Close your eyes and sense the energy in your home. See if there are any rooms or areas you feel drawn to. If you feel depressed, angry or uncomfortable in your home for no reason, ask your higher self and your energy radar to guide you to the places and spaces that most need clearing

- ✓ Regularly cleanse the energy in your home using sage to smudge or essential oils in a burner. Play sacred music as you work, and open the windows and doors for a while to allow the fresh, clean air to blow in, washing any lower energies harmlessly away on the cleansing breath of mother nature

- ✓ Spend three days eating only savoury food, allowing only the occasional green apple for sweetness and see what changes. Retrain yourself to prefer savoury and sour tastes such as green apples and lemon-water.

- ✓ Squirt lemon juice over everything – lemon juice can help to reduce sugar cravings and who knows, you might learn to love the taste

- ✓ Find other ways to comfort yourself, and learn to see food as fuel rather than a way to stuff down unpleasant feelings

- ✓ Strike food off the list of things you use to celebrate or reward yourself.

- ✓ The only butter in your house should be Shea butter

- ✓ Before you run to the shops to buy chocolate and sweeties, ask yourself what just happened? *Why am I suddenly doing this after weeks of abstinence?* Stop, breathe, clear your energy and reach for a green apple. At this point, your body just wants something, *anything*, to take away the pain and move it out of this horrible toxic state, replacing the stolen energy with some kind of sugar. Train yourself to reach for a green apple when these situations arise. You'll be shocked to see that it can actually work after a while

- ✓ Do as many things as you can to have fun without food and find fun people to do them with.

- ✓ Spend more time with people who have a healthier, non-addictive approach to food and nutrition. Watch and learn

- ✓ Find hobbies you feel passionate about, and which keep you too occupied to think about food

- ✓ Give yourself plenty of time to get ready for work and cultivate a habit of arriving at appointments early. It's much better to be too early and sit reading calmly while you wait, than to panic and end up taking the underground, getting trapped in a lift with a vampire or generally arriving in a stressed-out panic

- ✓ Stay away from angry, violent and argumentative people

- ✓ Join a dance class or take up another hobby that generates happy chemicals in your brain and allows you to shake of negative energy quickly

- ✓ Switch off the TV and mainstream radio as much as possible and fill your ears with positive, inspirational and education input

- ✓ As much as possible, weave little time and space treats and structures into your day, and build them into your life

- ✓ Take naps – guilt free

- ✓ Remember, there's no such thing as one chocolate bar! Chocolate is dead to you now!

- ✓ Learn to find a quiet place and breathe deeply. Sometimes it's our panic that drains us.

✓ Improve your time spent at work by considering your needs deeply and making notes about your non-negotiables, before making future career decisions. Don't be afraid to be very specific, when journaling to gain clarity about your dream job.

✓ Make a frequent practice of checking with yourself to see what has pulled you out of the vibrant stream of well-being and positive expectation.

✓ Take time to walk in nature, allowing the high vibrations of the earth, the trees, the sun and wind, to cleanse, refresh and renew you. Walk by the sea whenever you can and allow the sparkles to caress your skin and soothe your jangled nerves.

Now, go back and re-read the chapter on Things That Trigger Empaths into Overwhelm, to read the full and detailed explanations behind these tips again.

Enjoy!

Happy healing!